MW00874951

the Blessing

A Study in GENESIS 12-36

DONNA GAINES

JEAN STOCKDALE

DAYNA STREET

ANGIE WILSON

ABBEY DANE

The Blessing: A Study in Genesis 12–36

©2022 Bellevue Baptist Church

All rights reserved. No part of this publication may be reproduced, stored in a retrieval system or transmitted in any form by any means, electronic, mechanical, photocopy, recording, or otherwise, without the prior permission of the author, except as provided for by USA copyright law.

Cover and book design: Amanda Weaver

Original art on cover: Kristi Hall

Map design: Paige Warren

Editing: Dayna Street, Donita Barnwell, Melissa Bobo Hardee, Lauren Gooden, Paige Warren, Vera Sidhom, Lexie Patrick

Unless otherwise indicated, Scripture taken from the NEW AMERICAN STANDARD BIBLE. ® Copyright ©1960, 1962, 1968, 1971, 1973, 1975, 1977, 1995 by Lockman Foundation. Used by permission. www.Lockman.org

Contents

How to Use this Study

Welcome to *The Blessing: A Study in Genesis 12-36*! In this study, we will rewind history around 4000 years and meet the forefathers of our faith – Abraham, Isaac, and Jacob. As we travel with them, we will have front row seats to their failures and flaws. But, we will also discover the steadfast faith they have in God, a faith that sets the standard for what it means to be obedient. Throughout the lessons in this study, we will see God repeat the covenant promise to Abraham, Isaac, and Jacob, as all three are promised land, many descendants, and a blessing from the Lord. Along the way, we will notice that God uses defining moments in each man's life to refine his character and prepare him to accomplish His divine purpose. And as we get to know them, we will learn much about ourselves and the purpose God has for each of us as heirs of the blessing through His Son.

This study is designed to provide an opportunity for personal study throughout the week, leading up to small group discussion and large group teaching time once a week. Each weekly lesson is divided into five daily homework assignments. Four days will center on Bible study and personal application focused on the Genesis passage for that lesson. Then on the fifth day, we will practice being a person who blesses others. (And we will have lots of fun doing so!)

In your small group time each week, you will be able to connect with other women and build life-giving, sharpening relationships. As you meet together, be ready to share what God has shown you through His Word using the weekly studies as a guide. In the large group teaching time, you will be challenged by relevant, biblical instruction that will encourage you to stand firm on the truth of God's Word.

Join us in our study of Genesis 12-36 as we see God's redemptive plan forge ahead and point the way to its ultimate fulfillment through His Son, Jesus Christ. Most of all, get ready for a personal encounter with the God of Abraham, Isaac, and Jacob, and prepare to experience His transforming power at work in and through you.

the Blessing
A Study in GENESIS 12-36

The pitcher of God's blessing remains ever tilted over the lives of His children as He makes room for more grace – with a tenacity that will not let us go – with a contention that is always battling for our souls – with an intrusiveness that will not be shut out – with a love that will not let us go. [1]
~ Kent Hughes

To the average eye, it was simply a damaged piece of marble. The sculpture had been abandoned twice – once in 1464 by Agostino di Duccio and later by Antonio Rossellino in 1475. Both sculptors rejected the six-ton piece of marble due to its imperfections. Then for twenty-five years, the massive block of Carrera marble laid neglected in the courtyard of the Opera del Duomo in Florence, Italy. But in 1501, a twenty-six-year-old artist named Michelangelo di Lodovico Buonarroti Simoni saw something in the stone that others had not. And he determined to chip away at the piece of marble until the seemingly worthless slab reached its full potential. For close to three years, Michelangelo worked in secrecy. When it rained, he worked in the open courtyard in soaking wet clothes. He frequently forgot to eat and would work all hours of the day and night, sleeping little. When he did sleep, he would often lie down on the ground beside the emerging statue, fully clothed, including his boots.

Then, in January 1504, Michelangelo completed one of the most renowned masterpieces of Renaissance sculpture and what many consider the greatest statue ever sculpted by human hands – The David. The 17-foot-high sculpture portrays the decisive moment when David decided to fight Goliath, conveying the tension in his neck and his bulging veins. With his raised left hand, he drapes the sling over his shoulder, and in his right hand he holds a rock. Michelangelo used a technique called a "contrapposto twist" – where more weight is placed on one leg and the other is bent – in order to create the appearance of motion.

When asked how he fashioned such a beautiful statue from a piece of marble that others had labeled a worthless mess, Michelangelo explained that as he chiseled, he envisioned what he called the *immagine del cuore*, or "image of the heart." The young artist believed the masterpiece was already inside the stone. All he had to do was remove the excess stone that did not resemble David. Michelangelo didn't see what was; he saw what could be. He didn't see the flaws in the stone; he saw a masterpiece of strength and beauty. This magnificent sculpture is not a testament to the slab of marble; it is a testament to the creative genius of Michelangelo. [2]

All throughout Scripture, God uses flawed clay to accomplish His purposes. But the achievement is never a testament to the individual; it is always a testament to the greatness of God. And so it is with the three men whose life stories are told in Genesis 12-36. Abraham, Isaac, and Jacob are all imperfect men who follow a perfect God. Jehovah, the Creator-Sculptor, will masterfully chip away the stony places in their lives throughout their spiritual journey. Warren Wiersbe gives us a snapshot of the father-son-grandson trio that God uses to establish the nation of Israel:

> When they were frightened, they admitted it. When they were caught scheming, they suffered for it and learned from the pain. When they succeeded, they shared the blessing with others. When they prayed, they were desperate; and when they confessed sin, they were broken. In short, they were authentic, real, believable, down-to-earth people. Flawed? Of course! Occasionally bad examples? Certainly. Blessed of God? Abundantly! [3]

Through these three men, God's redemptive plan forges ahead. Even when they blow it big time. Although difficult for our human minds to comprehend, the sovereignty of God encompasses the free actions of human beings. As Proverbs 19:21 tells us, "Many are the plans in the mind of a man, but it is the purpose of the Lord that will stand" (ESV). In Genesis 12-36, God will give, and then graciously begin to unfold, the fulfillment of the covenant promise that His people will be numerous, will possess a land of their own, and will be a source of blessing to all the peoples of the world. Despite the sinful and disordered lives of Abraham, Isaac, and Jacob, God's promise stands. Such is the faithfulness of God. And through the sanctifying grace of God, His plan to return the earth to the way it was meant to be moves forward.

All throughout Scripture, God uses flawed clay to accomplish His purposes. But the achievement is never a testament to the individual; it is always a testament to the greatness of God.

Genesis – The Book of Beginnings

According to the custom in ancient times, the Jews named the first book of the Bible after the first word in the Hebrew text, *Bereshith*, which means "In the beginning." When the Old Testament was translated into Greek around 250 B.C., the title was rendered Genesis, a word that means "beginning." [4] Genesis is the book of beginnings – the beginning of the world, human history, the family, sin, and redemption.

This first book of the Bible is foundational to the rest of Scripture, and to every human life. It tells us who God is, who we are, how sin distorted the earth, and the plan God has to redeem humanity.

> *Genesis is the foundational book of the Bible, and the rest of*
> *Scripture is built upon what Moses wrote.* [5]
>
> ~ Warren Wiersbe

Genesis 1-11. The first eleven chapters of Genesis, primeval history, provide the earliest details of the Bible from the creation of the world in Genesis 1 to the Tower of Babel in Genesis 11. In Creation, God fashions man in His own image as His representative to fill and rule the earth (Genesis 1:26-28). Even after Adam and Eve sin, God gives the promise that the offspring of the woman will defeat the serpent and restore the earth (Genesis 3:15). The promise is traced through ten genealogies, *toledots*, that begin with Creation (2:4-4:26) and then move through the lives of key individuals: Adam (5:1-6:8), Noah (6:9-9:29), Noah's sons (10:1-11:19), Shem (11:10-26), Terah (11:27-25:11), Ishmael (25:12-18), Isaac (25:19-35:29), Esau (36:1-37:1), and Jacob (37:2-50:26). Genesis 1-11 can be summarized under three headings: Creation (Genesis 1-2), The Fall of Man (Genesis 3), and Man's Sinfulness (Genesis 4-11). Up to this point, God has dealt with His fallen creation on a universal scale. But neither massive flooding nor the scattering of humanity has stemmed the tide of evil in the world. So, God moves in a different way.

Genesis 12-36. The narrative of Genesis begins with the vast expanse of the universe and then narrows its scope to one man, a Mesopotamian sheep herder, his family, and their journey of faith. The individual stories of Abraham, Isaac, and Jacob demonstrate how the promise of Genesis 3:15 will be fulfilled. Sin has ruptured the perfect relationship between God and humanity, and now instead of thriving under the blessing God intended, humanity is yoked with the curse. But then God establishes His plan for redemption and blessing through a covenant with Abraham (12:1-3), reaffirms with Isaac (26:2-5; 24), then restates it with Jacob (28:10-15). Thus, Genesis sets the panoramic stage for God's plan to redeem the world through His Son, Jesus Christ.

Abraham, Isaac, and Jacob are known as the patriarchs, the line of men God used to establish the nation of Israel. Men, who we will find out, are a lot like us. Their faith walk is best described as a one step forward, two steps back progression. God will use defining moments in each of their lives to chip off their defects, strengthen their faith, and prepare them to be used to fulfill His plan that will pave the way for salvation for all. More importantly, as we study these three men, we will learn much about the God they served. Their lives will reveal a God who loves us unconditionally and infinitely, guides us with His faithful presence and omniscient plan, holds us personally accountable, and blesses us beyond our wildest imagination!

The Author. Genesis is set within the larger collection of five books in the Bible known as the Pentateuch. Although books in the Old Testament rarely include a byline, the authorship of Genesis (as well as the rest of the Pentateuch) is generally attributed to Moses. Both the Old and New Testament give affirmation that Moses is the writer of the Pentateuch:

- "Then the Lord said to Moses, 'Write this in a book as a memorial and recite it to Joshua…'" (Exodus 17:14a).

- "It came about, when Moses finished writing the words of this law in a book until they were complete…" (Deuteronomy 31:24).

- "…according to what is written in the book of the Law of Moses…" (2 Kings 14:6).

- "For Moses writes that the man who practices the righteousness which is based on law shall live by that righteousness" (Romans 10:5).

- "But to this day whenever Moses is read…" (2 Corinthians 3:15).

Even more significantly, 1500 years after it is written, Jesus confirms the Mosaic authorship of Genesis:

- "Now He said to them, 'These are My words which I spoke to you while I was still with you, that all things which are written about Me in the Law of Moses and the Prophets and the Psalms must be fulfilled'" (Luke 24:44).

- "Do not think that I will accuse you before the Father; the one who accuses you is Moses, in whom you have set your hope. For if you believed Moses, you would believe Me, for he wrote about Me. But if you do not believe his writings, how will you believe My words?" (John 5:45-47).

- "Did not Moses give you the Law, and yet none of you carries out the Law? Why do you seek to kill Me…If a man receives circumcision on the Sabbath so that the Law of Moses will not be broken, are you angry with Me because I made an entire man well on the Sabbath?" (John 7:19, 23).

Of course, Moses lived after the events recorded in Genesis. So, how did he know about what happened before his time? Most theologians believe that Moses' knowledge of some of the events in Genesis came from oral traditions and/or well-preserved written documents from the patriarchs. The genealogy of Exodus 6:16-20 tells us that Moses was the great-great grandson of Jacob, so it is likely that he heard many of the events in Genesis as a young boy. Other things, such as the account of Creation, he would only have known by supernatural revelation from God. As is seen throughout the book of

Exodus, "Moses talked to God and then God talked to Moses and communicated knowledge that he would not have known otherwise." [6]

So the LORD spoke to Moses face to face as a man speaks to his friend.
Exodus 33:11a, NKJV

Date and Setting. An exact date for the writing of the Pentateuch is not given, but it is believed that Moses most likely wrote it during the fifteenth century B.C. in the wilderness of Sinai, between the time he led the Israelites out of bondage in Egypt and his death. Genesis provides a history of the Israelites forefathers – their backgrounds, their journeys, and their covenants with God. Chuck Swindoll writes, "Because the events contained in the rest of the Pentateuch are responses to the promises of God found in Genesis, such a history of God's interaction with their ancestors would have provided encouragement and inspiration to the former slaves seeking freedom and prosperity in the Promised Land." [7] Thus, Genesis serves as a historical preface to the covenant God made with the nation of Israel. In essence, it is a written record of what He has done on their behalf and a reminder that they are to obey the terms of His covenant with them.

The Blessing

Blessing is the bestowing of privilege, right, responsibility, or favor upon some portion of the creation, by God or by one whom He has blessed. In relation to humanity, to be blessed is to be one of God's own people with all the benefit that brings: in other words, the blessing of God is His relational presence in one's life. [8]
~ Matt Champlin

A blessing is any act of God that brings Him glory by accomplishing His will and helping people to grow and do His will. [9]
~ Warren Wiersbe

From the first chapter to the last chapter of Genesis, God blesses humanity. The words "bless" or "blessing" are used more than 80 times throughout the fifty chapters, and scholars have estimated that Genesis contains nearly one sixth of all scriptural references to blessing. [10] In Genesis 1, God blesses mankind (1:22; 28), but then sin enters the world and they lose the blessing (Genesis 3). In Genesis 12, God moves to restore the blessing through one couple, Abram and Sarai, and their offspring. Prior to Genesis 12, "blessing" is only mentioned three times after the completion of Creation (2:4).

Genesis 12-36 points the way forward to the ultimate fulfillment of God's redemption plan for man through His Son, Jesus Christ.

The curse, on the other hand, has had a monopolizing presence in humanity. But then, God speaks to Abram, and within the two verses of Genesis 12:2-3, He blesses him five times. James McKeown points out, "The blessing of Abraham is strategically positioned between the primeval narrative and the patriarchal narratives so that it marks a turning point from an agenda dominated by cursing to one dominated by blessing." [11] However, the curse is not terminated with the Abrahamic blessing: God promises Abram, the blessed one, "the one who curses you I will curse" (Genesis 12:3). It will not be until the consummation of history, when the Lamb of God takes His place upon the throne, that there will "no longer be any curse" (Revelation 22:3). But from the turning point in Genesis 12, "the pitcher of God's blessing" moves to the forefront and tilts over those who walk with Him, showering them with grace, mercy, and love, even in their most undeserving moments.

Genesis 12-36 points the way forward to the ultimate fulfillment of God's redemption plan for man through His Son, Jesus Christ. As Paul tells us, "if you belong to Christ, then you are Abraham's descendants, heirs according to promise" (Galatians 3:29). In Christ, you are an heir to the promises God made to Abraham. You are a recipient of the blessing, the beneficiary of "every spiritual blessing in the heavenly places in Christ" (Ephesians 1:3). In Him, "all things belong to you, whether...the world or life or death, or things present or things to come; all things [all the promises!] belong to you, and you belong to Christ; and Christ belongs to God" (1 Corinthians 3:21-23, emphasis mine). What blessings are ours in Him!

So, let's get ready to rewind history around 4000 years and meet the forefathers of our faith – Abraham, Isaac, and Jacob. We will see these men and their families cross deserts, ride camels, dwell in tents, acquire wealth, suffer childlessness, receive the blessing of God, and experience the glory of God. We will find that Scripture does not airbrush the lives of the patriarchs, as we will have front row seats to their failures and flaws. But we will also see their faith in God, a faith that will challenge and inspire us.

More than anything else, our prayer is that through this study, we will come to know the God of Abraham, Isaac, and Jacob more intimately and encounter Him in a life-changing way, as He chips away the excess stone in our lives that does not look like His Son with a "tenacity that will not let us go," a "contention that is always battling for our souls," an "intrusiveness that will not be shut out," and His "love that will not let us go." [12]

ABRAM IS BLESSED
Genesis 12-13

Jesus didn't die to keep us safe. He died to make us dangerous. Faithfulness is not holding the fort. It's storming the gates of hell. The will of God is not an insurance plan. It's a daring plan. The complete surrender of your life to the cause of Christ isn't radical. It's normal. It's time to quit living as if the purpose of life is to arrive safely at death. It's time to go all in and all out for the All in All. [1]

~ Mark Batterson

Some moments are permanently etched upon our minds. One morning, I was standing in the kitchen when our oldest son, Jonathan, who was in his first semester of law school, began to walk down the stairs with a piece of paper from a yellow legal pad in his hand. He paused for a moment on the stairs and taped the paper to the stairwell wall in front of him. He then came into the kitchen, grabbed his lunch, gave me a hug, and left for school. Curious, I walked up the stairs and turned around to see what "art" was now adorning our stairwell. What I found were these nine words, "Life begins at the end of your comfort zone." Law school was the land of the unfamiliar. New school. New professors. New peers. New academic discipline. And this was the environment he was to spend most of his waking hours in for the next three years. Not only was it unfamiliar, it was uncomfortable. The word he would have probably used was grueling. Moving forward would require a risk. But one step at a time, one day at a time, he kept at it.

More than a decade has passed since that staircase moment. Jonathan has long since finished law school. He is married, with his own family, practicing law in another state. But that message written on the yellow legal page still hangs on the stairwell in our home. Why? Because sometimes his mom needs to be reminded that Jesus isn't concerned about my comfort or ease. What He wants is my obedience.

The poem, "Make Me Thy Fuel," written by Amy Carmichael (1867-1951), a missionary to India for fifty-three years, captures well what it means to live in complete surrender to the cause of Christ:

> From prayer that asks that I may be
> Sheltered from winds that beat on Thee,
> From fearing when I should aspire,
> From faltering when I should climb higher,
> From silken self, O Captain, free
> Thy soldier who would follow Thee.
>
> From subtle love of softening things,
> From easy choices, weakenings,
> Not thus are spirits fortified,
> Not this way went the Crucified;
> From all that dims Thy Calvary,
> O Lamb of God, deliver me.
>
> Give me the love that leads the way,
> The faith that nothing can dismay,
> The hope no disappointments tire,
> The passion that will burn like fire;
> Let me not sink to be a clod;
> Make me Thy fuel, Flame of God. [2]

Our "silken self" and our "love of softening things" keep us chained to comfort and rob us from effectiveness for God. As we journey through the story of Abraham, we will discover that there are

Jesus isn't concerned about my comfort or ease. What He wants is my obedience.

no limits to what God can do through a person who is fully surrendered to Him. When God calls Abraham, he leaves behind the ease of the life he has known to step into an unknown future. But when he gets outside of his comfort zone, he finds the life that God has for him is more than he could have ever imagined.

And so will we.

Genesis 12:1-3

When we first meet Abraham on the pages of Scripture, four centuries have passed since the human race became so corrupt that God wiped out all but Noah's family in the flood. Ten generations after this fresh start, the human population has bounced back, but its moral condition has not improved. Kent Hughes gives us insight into the spiritual darkness of the times:

> During the ten generations from Noah through Shem to [Abraham] the whole family of earth had played out its future and had nowhere to go. The culture of Babel, though dispersed, had triumphed. There was no foreseeable future other than darkness. And there was certainly no human power to invent a future. Mankind was hopelessly lost, except for the distant promise to Shem that blessing would come through his line (cf. 9:26, 27). [3]

God could have abandoned mankind to its own self-destructive devices. Chuck Swindoll points out that God "was not morally compelled to rescue humanity from the evil it created and perpetuated." [4] Yet, instead of destroying mankind, He sets into motion a plan to redeem the world. And His plan begins with one man – Abraham.

At the end of Genesis 11, Moses introduces Abraham, or Abram as he is known as for the first 99 years of his life. His story is so significant that "the Spirit of God devotes 25 percent of the book of Genesis to its details." [5] In his introduction to this hero of the faith, Moses fills in some of his family ties and presents the cast of characters who will play important roles in Abram's story.

1. Read Genesis 11:27-32 and fill in the following biographical information on Abram:

Abram's father is _____.

His two brothers are _____ and _____.

Abram's wife is named _____.

His nephew, the son of his deceased brother, Haran, is _____.

Terah and his family have settled in Ur of the Chaldeans, an area colonized by the descendants of Noah's son, Ham. In the fertile plains of Chaldea, the sons of Ham "built towns of baked clay, erected temples, of which the ruins remain to this day, and cultivated the arts of civilized life to an extent unknown elsewhere." [6] The land of the Chaldeans, also known as Mesopotamia, is called the cradle of civilization, because it was the geographic area where people first gathered, built cities, and established societies.

2. Circle Abram's hometown of Ur on the map below.

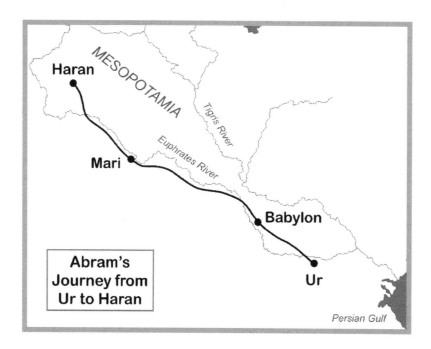

Ur was located in modern-day Iraq and was a busy port on the Euphrates River. A massive rectangular pyramidal structure called a ziggurat contained the temple of Nanna and towered 70 feet above the city. Excavations at the beginning of the twentieth century uncovered the ziggurat in its entirety and the structure still dominates the landscape today. [7] The residents of Ur were idolators who worshiped a number of mythical gods who were ruled by Nanna, the moon god, whom they recognized as the "creator of all things." [8]

Archeologists have discovered that the city was surrounded by walls and had streets that were carefully laid out. At the time Abram lived in Ur, the thriving city was home to more than 60,000 people. The municipality was known for its wool industry that produced and exported clothes and carpets. Business records that have been discovered show that due to its close proximity to the Persian Gulf, Ur established a lucrative international trade industry with merchants from India and Africa. Consequently, the residents of Ur enjoyed a prosperous lifestyle and became one of the most advanced ancient civilizations known to man. [9]

Into this Hamite civilization enters a tribe of shepherds led by Terah, a descendant of one of Noah's other sons, Shem. Terah and his family settled in the pastures outside of Ur's walls. Although their forefather, Shem, knew the one true God, Terah and his family have succumbed to the culture around them and abandoned their godly heritage.

3. In Joshua 24:2, who does Joshua say Terah, Abraham, and Nahor worshiped (served)?

Abram, like his father and brother, is a pagan idolator living in a pagan city when God calls him to a new way of life. The Genesis 11 account does not provide the details of God's revelation of Himself to Abram. However, it is apparently so powerful that Terah is not only convinced to go along, but he also leads the family pilgrimage out from Ur.

4. After they leave Ur, where do they go? (Genesis 11:31)

5. Look back at the map on page 16 and circle the town of Haran.

Just like Ur, Haran is a town devoted to the worship of the moon god. Located on the frontier of the Babylonian Empire, Haran becomes the first stop on their pilgrimage, and they remain there until Terah dies.

If we only had the Genesis 11-12 account, we might conclude that God called Abram after Terah died. However, the rest of Scripture tells us differently.

6. Read Genesis 15:7, Nehemiah 9:7, and Acts 7:2-4. Where is Abram living when God calls him?

In the deep darkness of Ur, Abram sees the glory of God. He hears God's call. As Derek Kidner notes, "The history of redemption, like that of creation, begins with God speaking." [10] And in response, although he is middle-aged, prosperous, settled, and a pagan idolator, Abram leaves the life of comfort he has known, steps out in faith, and obeys God partially by moving from Ur to Haran. While we do not know for sure why Abram stops in Haran, most commentators believe that it has something to do with Terah.

F.B. Meyer ponders:

> Was it that the old man was too weary for further journeyings? Did he like Haran too well to leave it? Did Terah's heart and flesh fail as he looked out on the far expanse of level sand, behind which the sun set in lurid glory every night? In any case, he would go no further on the pilgrimage, and it appears that for as long as fifteen years, Abraham's obedience was on hold. [11]

Read Genesis 12:1-3.

7. What three things does God tell Abram to go from? (v. 1)

-

-

-

8. Where does God tell Abram to go? (v. 1)

This would have been a big step of obedience for Abram. Imagine the conversation with Sarai when he tells her that they are headed to an unknown destination where they know no one. But as the writer of Hebrews tells us, "By faith Abraham, when he was called, obeyed by going out to a place which he was to receive for an inheritance; and he went out, not knowing where he was going" (Hebrews 11:8). Abram's outward obedience reveals his inward faith. Faith and obedience are inseparable to God.

9. God makes 5 promises to Abram in verses 1-3. What does God tell Abram He will do?

- I will _____.

- I will _____.

- And _____.

- I will _____.

- I will _____.

These verses of blessing are known as the Abrahamic Covenant that will be confirmed in Genesis 15 in a covenant ceremony. Did you notice the progression of God's blessing? Abram is blessed. Then Abram's name is used as a blessing. Then those who bless Abram are blessed. Then all the families of the world will be blessed.

As we will see throughout our study, God's blessings will begin in Abram's lifetime. However, the ultimate fulfillment of the promise will come through Christ, the seed of Abram, as Paul makes clear: "The Scripture, foreseeing that God would justify the Gentiles by faith, preached the gospel beforehand to Abraham, saying, 'All the nations will be blessed in you.' So then those who are of faith are blessed with Abraham, the believer" (Galatians 3:8-9). And dear believing friend, that includes you!

As you close your time in God's Word today, spend a few moments reflecting on the many ways God has blessed you.

Father, thank You for the many ways You have blessed me.
Thank You for redeeming my life and giving me eternal life through
Jesus. Forgive me for the times I have selfishly enjoyed my blessings
with no thought as to how I can bless others. Help me to envision myself in
the lineage of Abraham, blessed to be a blessing. As You have forgiven me,
may I also be forgiving. As You have given me grace, may I be a grace giver
to others. Use me today as Your instrument in the lives of others. Amen.

day two

Genesis 12:4-9

When God bestows the promise of blessing upon Abram, the threads of redemptive history begin to take shape as God sets His salvation plan for man into motion. It is doubtful that Abram understands the full ramifications of God's blessing, for it will be another 2,000 years before the hope for the world is purchased through Christ's death on the cross and the empty tomb. Abram could have responded in a number of ways to God's call. He could have clung to the comfort of familiarity. He could have calculated the risk and opted for the safe surroundings of the known. But instead, He goes all in. He leaves the familiar behind and begins an incredible journey of faith with God.

1. What are some ways God has called you to step out of your comfort zone and learn to live by faith?

Trusting God is not always easy, is it? Swindoll writes, "If every missionary looked for comfort or convenience or familiarity, missions would collapse overnight. Ministries would fold, and charities would close up shop." [12] And we would miss out on God's purpose for our lives. Do you trust God enough with your future to obey Him immediately in the present?

Read Genesis 12:4-5.

2. How old is Abram when he leaves Haran for Canaan? (v. 4)

By the time most people are 75, they are set in their ways. They are living where they are going to live. The thought of change causes an emotional upheaval. But Abram silences the voice of common sense, refuses to be swayed by what people might think or say, and packs up. And "the story of Abram's seedling faith becoming a fully mature, fruit-bearing tree" begins. [13] Abram leaves behind the comfortable life of a city dweller to become a nomad. What drives Abram? What will keep him going through difficult days and desolate nights? Belief. Abram believes. He knows Whom he has believed and is persuaded that He is able to guard everything which he has entrusted to Him until that day (2 Timothy 1:12). He also believes that what God has promised, He will perform. In the words of Howard Hendricks, "Faith is the hand that turns promises into performance." [14] Because of Abram's great faith, he is "content to sail with sealed orders because of unwavering confidence in the love and wisdom of the Lord High Admiral." [15]

And so, Abram's caravan sets out. Camels loaded down, sheep bleating. Abram, Sarai, his nephew, Lot, and all of the others who go with them begin an 800-mile sojourn south to the land of Canaan. The letter to the Hebrews gives us insight into Abram's relationship to the Promised Land, "By faith he went to live in the land of promise, as in a foreign land, living in tents with Isaac and Jacob, heirs with him of the same promise. For he was looking forward to the city that has foundations, whose designer and builder is God" (Hebrews 11:9-10, ESV). Abram never loses sight of God's call. He believes God for the future and that belief keeps him detached from the world, just as faith will "always detach God's people from grounding their lives too deeply in the present." [16]

How different that is from our natural desires that have been infiltrated by our culture! We long for security, a place to settle down. The voices around us tell us to hunker down and protect ourselves and our families. But God's Word tells us otherwise.

3. What instruction does God give us in Matthew 6:33 and Colossians 3:1-4?

4. Take just a few moments and honestly reflect. Would you say that you are living a detached life or an attached life? Is your mind set on Christ or are you so attached to the present that the things of the world have dimmed your view of Him?

Read Genesis 12:6-9.

When Abram reaches Canaan, the land of promise, he travels across it from one end to the other, symbolically taking "possession of it for his descendants, lingering at holy places, and building altars."[17] Warren Wiersbe helps us apply the spiritual significance of Canaan to our own lives:

> It is a picture of the believer claiming his or her inheritance by faith. God has appointed a "Canaan" for each of His children (Ephesians 2:10), and it is obtained only by faith. Claiming your inheritance involves tests and temptations, challenges and battles, but God is able to see you through (Philippians 1:6). [18]

5. When Abram gets to Canaan, where does he stop first? (v. 6)

Shechem is the geographical center of the Promised Land. Because of its location and vital intersection, Shechem is often mentioned in the Bible. Many years later, Abraham will purchase a burial plot for Sarah here (Genesis 23:16-20). His grandson, Jacob, will also buy land in Shechem (Genesis 33:18-20) and apparently dig a well on it, because John 4 tells us that Jesus was sitting by Jacob's well when He met the Samaritan woman and gave her living water so that she would never thirst again. [19]

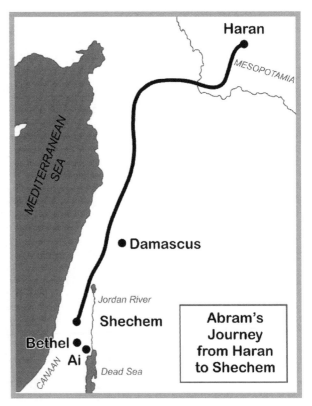

In Genesis 12:6, Moses records that Canaanites are living in the land, an indication of the opposition that will be a reality to Abram as he continues his faith journey. Hughes explains that the oak tree at Moreh is the place "where the Canaanites assembled to hear the oracles that soothsayers received from the rustling of the leaves." [20] Historical records tell us that the "Canaanites had shrines in groves of oak trees, and Moreh may have been one of their cult centers." [21] Right in the heart of the land God has promised to Abram, idolatry is thriving. But right there as Abram is camped near this pagan shrine, God appears to him and gives him a fourth promise.

6. What promise does God give to Abram in Shechem? (v. 7)

In Genesis 12:1-3, God promised Abram a great people, a great name, and a great blessing. Now He promises a great land. The promise of land is part of the Abrahamic Covenant. Notice that God doesn't promise the land to Abram, but to his descendants. This is not only a promise that the land will eventually belong to his descendants, but also that he will have descendants. And to childless Abram and Sarai, the promise of land and descendants likely prompts a million questions about how these things will happen.

7. But instead of asking questions, how does Abram respond to God's promise? (v. 7)

Abram worships. Just like his forefather Noah did when he stepped off of the Ark, Abram builds an altar to God to worship Him. And then he leads his entourage some twenty-one miles to the south, halfway between Bethel, to the west, and Ai, to the east, and pitches his tent. There, he once again builds an altar. Abram has now built an altar to the Lord at Shechem and east of Bethel. He will also build altars in Hebron and at Mount Moriah (Genesis 13:18; 22:9). Hughes comments, "How beautiful— the only architecture that remained from Abram's life were altars." [22] What a difference between Abram and the tower builders at Babel! At Babel, they built to "make for ourselves a name" (Genesis 11:4); Abram builds to make great the name of God.

While Abram's tent marks him as a "stranger and pilgrim" who is aware that he does not belong to this world (Hebrews 11:9), the altars he builds to worship the true and living God indicate that his citizenship is in Heaven.

8. Reread Genesis 12:4-9 and make note of the verbs used to describe Abram's life.

- Verse 4 –

- Verse 5 –

- Verse 6 –

- Verse 8 –

- Verse 9 –

Step-by-step, Abram keeps moving forward. If we have faith, our actions and activity will correspond with what we believe. As James tells us, "Don't just listen to God's Word. You must do what it says. Otherwise, you are only fooling yourselves" (James 1:22, NLT). A faith that does not keep walking is a faith that will eventually become too weak to stand.

Verse 9 tells us that Abram continues on in his journey of faith and leads his caravan south toward the region of the Negev. As they go, I can almost hear the song they sing:

> I have decided to follow Yahweh,
> I have decided to follow Yahweh,
> I have decided to follow Yahweh,
> No turning back, no turning back.
>
> Tho' none go with me, I still will follow,
> Tho' none go with me, I still will follow,
> Tho' none go with me, I still will follow,
> No turning back, no turning back. [23]

Can you honestly sing those words? Are you moving forward in faith? If not, what is holding you back? Obedience really isn't that complicated. Don't let the lack of details keep you from stepping out. As the Nike commercial says, "Just Do It!" God is giving you an opportunity to grow your faith. Trust Him.

God will make this happen, for He who calls you is faithful.
1 Thessalonians 5:24, NLT

Genesis 12:10-13:4

When we left Abram yesterday, he was continuing his journey in Canaan and was on his way to the Negev, the desert region in the southern part of Canaan. Things have been going well for Abram. He is growing in his faith and has an intimate relationship with God. Life is good. And then, he comes face to face with a test.

A severe famine sweeps across the Negev region.

Read Genesis 12:10.

The Hebrew word used for famine in Genesis 12:10 simply means "hunger." [24] While we don't know if the famine was the result of a drought or a crop failure, what we do know is that the people living in the area were hungry. And so were their herds and flocks!

All eyes are upon Abram. Will he just allow his people and animals to starve to death? I can imagine what the cynics traveling with him have to say, "Are you sure this is the land of promise, Abram? Did you just bring us this far to die?" Swindoll gives us insight into what the famine experience would have been like for Abram:

> As a newcomer, Abram may not have known how frequently food became scarce in this region. Having come from a part of the world known as the Fertile Crescent, he may have expected lush grass for his flocks along with bumper crops of wheat and barley. Compared to the land on the banks of the Euphrates, the Negev looked like a waste land. [25]

So, Abram has a decision to make. He can either stay in the land God has called him to and trust that God will provide, or he can leave the land and look to man to provide.

1. What does Abram do when famine hits the Negev? (v. 10)

Abram does the natural thing and shifts into survival mode. He stops believing in the supernatural promises of God, and he packs up his caravan and heads to Egypt. Think about that. God has appeared to Abram. God has spoken to him. Abram has built altars and called upon the name of the Lord. But for the first time in his faith walk, he is tested. And when that happens, he ignores the promises of God and goes to Egypt for help. His trust in God shifts to trusting in man.

In Scripture, Egypt is symbolic of the world. Meyer explains the spiritual ramifications of Abram's choice:

> In the figurative language of Scripture, Egypt stands for an alliance with the world…. [Abram] acted simply on his own judgement. He looked at his difficulties and became paralyzed with fear. He grasped at the first means of deliverance that suggested itself, much as a drowning man will catch at a straw. And thus, without taking counsel of his heavenly Protector, [Abram] went down to Egypt. [26]

Abram does not deny God, he merely forgets Him. And Abram's faithless decision to go down to Egypt is a precursor to a chain of events that he is not prepared for.

Note: Abram's choice will become a pattern for the Israelites. Later on, his grandson Jacob will move his family to Egypt when another famine hits. And centuries later, this pattern will result in the enslavement of the Israelites to the Egyptians. Our choices always have far-reaching consequences, don't they?

How often do we act just like Abram? Peeling back our own pattern of behavior when we are being tested, Hughes writes, "Trials come, and we automatically go into survival mode. We scheme, we prognosticate, we run through the 'what ifs,' we shore up our position, we pile sandbags. And God? Oh yes. We ask Him to bless our ways." [27] Oh my.

Once he arrives in Egypt, Abram's shift in trust spirals down pretty quickly as he is greeted with a new set of problems.

Read Genesis 12:11-16.

2. Summarize the situation Abram now finds himself facing. (vv. 11-16)

Abram has taken his eyes off of God and fear has taken over his life. It has mutated from fear of starvation to fear for his life. So, he concocts a plan. Actually, "scheme" is a better word.

3. Make a list of all the things you can think of that are wrong with Abram's scheme.

Abram's scheme is built around a lie that he rationalizes. After all, Sarai is his half-sister (Genesis 20:12). He can satisfy his conscience in saying truthfully that he is Sarai's brother. However, Abram knows well how the Egyptians will interpret the story he will tell them, and he is likely pretty pleased with himself for being so clever. But he has forgotten about one thing. Pharaoh.

While the ordinary Egyptian man would have negotiated with Abram as Sarai's guardian (allowing him time to devise an out), Pharaoh, the ruler of Egypt, just takes her. And Abram's scheme disintegrates on the spot.

Abram's beautiful wife is taken into Pharaoh's harem, and Abram's anxiety moves into overdrive. What will happen to Sarai? Has he lost her for good? Swindoll notes that "fortunately, ancient marriage rituals included a waiting period long enough to ensure that a bride wasn't already pregnant. So Sarai lived inside the palace but was isolated from contact by anyone, including the king." [28] Perhaps that offers Abram some consolation, but the clock is ticking.

And then to make matters worse, gifts begin to arrive at Abram's tent. Egypt's Amazon delivery service starts dropping off wedding gifts (think dowry) from Pharaoh. Sheep, oxen, donkeys, servants. Abram is moving on up in Egyptian life, but without his beloved wife. And the only person he can blame is himself.

Let's pause here and recognize that Abram is not the only one who struggles with faithlessness. It's easy to trust God when things are going well. But when a famine strikes in our lives, how often do we turn to our own means and schemes to try to fix the problem? And for a while, it may seem that our devices are working. Until they don't.

At this point in the saga, that is where Abram finds himself.

Read Genesis 12:17-20.

Verse 17 is the first mention of God since Abram has crossed the border from the land of promise into Egypt.

4. How does God intervene on behalf of Sarai? (v. 17)

Although Abram has taken his eyes off of God, God has not lost sight of Abram and Sarai. In spite of Abram's faithlessness, God remains faithful. God sends a plague to Pharaoh that moves throughout the palace. Somehow, Pharaoh discovers the truth about Sarai already being married. Then Abram is hauled in before Pharaoh and interrogated. Pharaoh pelts Abram with questions that all sound pretty much like, "Why didn't you just tell me the truth?" Meanwhile, Abram just stands there silent

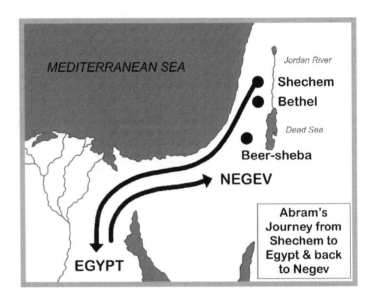

"and embarrassed in the presence of the indignant king. What a tremendous opportunity for personal witness to the living God he had lost because he had compromised the truth." [29] Although Abram should have been morally superior to the pagan, polytheistic king, he fails on all counts and forfeits any prospect of pointing Pharaoh to the one true God. I just have to wonder – how often do our own failures misrepresent the God we say we serve?

And then just like that, Abram and Sarai aren't just thrown out of the palace, they are expelled from the country.

Read Genesis 13:1-4.

With the Egyptian episode in his rearview, Abram crosses back into the Promised Land, wiser and wealthier. In fact, Genesis 13:2 says that he is "very wealthy." God has graciously blessed Abram in spite of his failure. Will he handle prosperity any differently than he did adversity?

As Abram heads northeast into Canaan with Sarai, Lot, his newly acquired herds, flocks, and servants (including a handmaid named Hagar), he is retracing his steps back to Bethel, to the place he never should have left, to the altar where he had called upon the name of the Lord. By now, Abram has learned that faith isn't just believing in the existence of God, it is living a life that trusts and honors Him.

Are you prepared for the next time you face a famine in your life? As James tells us, we are to "consider it a sheer gift, friends, when tests and challenges come at you from all sides. You know that under pressure, your faith-life is forced into the open and shows its true colors. So don't try to get out of anything prematurely. Let it do its work so you become mature and well-developed, not deficient in any way" (James 1:2-4, MSG). When the famine comes – and it will – don't try to bypass it, don't try to short circuit it, don't try to side-step it. Instead, trust God and walk through it. And just watch what He will do in and through you in the process!

5. What are some scriptures you stand upon when you go through times of testing?

Let us not be surprised when we have to face difficulties. When the wind blows hard on a tree, the roots stretch and grow the stronger, let it be so with us. Let us not be weaklings, yielding to every wind that blows, but strong in spirit to resist. [30]
~ Amy Carmichael

day four

Genesis 13:5-18

High up in the Rocky Mountains, about 60 miles west of Denver, Colorado, is a point along the Continental Divide where the waters of a stream separate and head in different directions. While it may seem inconsequential whether a drop of water goes to the right or the left there, it is far from that. This 11,990-foot pass, known as Loveland Pass, is the dividing point for the watersheds that flow into the Pacific and Atlantic Oceans. If a drop of water goes to the west, it will eventually flow into the Colorado River, which empties into the Gulf of California and the Pacific Ocean. If a drop heads east, it will wind up in the Mississippi River, which flows to the Gulf of Mexico and the Atlantic Ocean. Two drops of water. Two different destinations. One turning point that makes a huge difference.

Our choices in life are just like that. Even a seemingly small decision can set into motion a sequence of events that impact your life, the lives of your children, your grandchildren, and generations to follow. And that is exactly what we will see happen with Abram's nephew, Lot.

Read Genesis 13:5-9.

Even a seemingly small decision can set into motion a sequence of events that impact your life, the lives of your children, your grandchildren, and generations to follow.

Up until this point in the story, all we really know about Lot is that his father, Haran, has died and that Abram, his uncle, has taken him under his wing, much like a surrogate. Do you remember when the Lord told Abram to leave his extended family behind in Genesis 12:1? But who does he wind up taking with him? His father and his nephew. Abram's lack of complete obedience is costly. His father, Terah, ends up holding up Abram's journey to the Promised Land for years. And although Lot has not yet caused him any issues, that is about to change.

1. What conflict arises between Abram and Lot? (vv. 5-7)

When Abram prospers, Lot benefits as well, accumulating flocks, herds, and tents. Additional flocks and herds require more food, more water, and more space. In a land that is recovering from a famine, that is a problem in the making. Prosperity has driven a wedge between Abram and Lot. As the situation escalates, their herdsmen begin to quarrel with each other, and an all-out range war, western movie style, seems imminent if nothing changes. And not only that, but apparently their enemies (the Canaanites and the Perizzites) have noticed the family feud.

When problems arise in relationships, it is easy for something that is really pretty small to accelerate quickly. But when we keep the relationship bigger than the problem, we will find ways to approach the problem so that the relationship is stronger once the issue is resolved. [31]

With his newly recharged faith, Abram takes the initiative and decides that it is best for he and Lot to go their separate ways. Solomon may have been thinking about Abram's example when he wrote, "The beginning of strife is like letting out water, so abandon the quarrel before it breaks out" (Proverbs 17:14). For Abram, his relationship with his nephew is more important than the conflict at hand.

2. What words would you use to describe Abram's approach with Lot? (vv. 8-9)

Hughes helps us to understand just how gracious Abram is with Lot:

> Abram, as the older man and the leader of the faith expedition, the one to whom the promises were made, could have appealed to his position, which was unassailable in Semitic culture. But he did not. Confident and unthreatened, he was selfless and generous—"Take your choice, my nephew and brother." [32]

Instead of demanding his due, Abram forgoes his rights in the interest of reconciliation.

Abram and Lot represent the two ways we approach problems in life. We either map out our world focusing on the problems to be solved or the people to be loved. Those who fixate on the problems to be solved are motivated by fear, and "by default lock on to whatever is scary or potentially bad in their environment, and that is what gets all of their attention." [33] However, those who concentrate on the people to be loved map out their life in terms of the good they see in people. They are masters at expressing appreciation, and they intentionally dwell on "whatever is true, whatever is honorable, whatever is right, whatever is pure, whatever is lovely, whatever is of good repute" (Philippians 4:8).

It is not that they ignore problems. In fact, they are expert problem solvers, because they approach them relationally and make sure that the relationship stays bigger than the problem. [34] Abram falls into this second group that is motivated by love, while Lot, on the other hand, is driven by fear.

Read Genesis 13:10-13.

3. What are some words you would use to describe Lot's choice? (vv. 10-13)

Lot is focused on the problem at hand and makes his choice by sight. Hughes elaborates,

> The language makes it clear that Lot intensely surveyed the Jordan Valley—"Lot lifted up his eyes and saw"—he took it all in. There scarce could be more lavish and evocative allusions than Eden and Egypt. The great river that flowed from Eden divided into four famous headwaters that watered Mesopotamia. The Nile was the life of Egypt. Lot saw the well-watered plain as paradise—though the very references to Eden and Egypt themselves also foreshadowed judgment. And, of course, the parenthetical "This was before the LORD destroyed Sodom and Gomorrah" is ominous. But what Lot saw with his eyes was stupendous—a verdant plain brightly dotted with inviting cities. [35]

The lush appearance of the land is alluring to Lot. And given his fear motivation and scarcity mindset, he makes the choice he believes will set him up for even greater prosperity. Sadly, the decision he makes will be the worst mistake of his life.

Lot lives by sight, but Abram lives by faith. Abram is undaunted when Lot chooses the premium land for his own. What a difference between this Abram and the one who was obsessed with his own self-protection in Egypt! He has matured in his faith, and he is not concerned about his unknown future because he is trusting in a known God.

Read Genesis 13:14-18.

After Lot goes his way, Abram has another meeting with the Lord. Wiersbe gives further insight into the contrast between Lot and Abram:

> Lot had lifted up his eyes and seen what the world had to offer; now God invited Abram to lift up his eyes and see what Heaven had to offer. Lot chose a piece of land, which he finally lost, but God gave Abram the whole land, which still belongs to him and his descendants. Lot had said, "I will take." God had said to Abram, "I will give." What a contrast! [36]

God then reiterates His promise to Abram.

4. Compare God's statement of promise in Genesis 13:14-18 with His original promise in Genesis 12:1-3. What information does God add when He restates His promise?

Let's not allow familiarity with this story to dull our senses to what Abram must have experienced. Place yourself in his sandals. Imagine the fullness of his heart as God once again promises him not only all the land to the north, south, east, and west, but also assures him that he will have descendants. As he tours the land and the goodness of God begins to sink in, I have to imagine that Abram is overcome with joy and gratitude. I can almost hear him humming a song of praise as he packs up his tents and loads up the camels to move yet once again.

5. What does Abram do when he gets to Hebron? (v. 18)

Once again, we see Abram worshiping. While he is growing closer and closer to God, Lot is inching closer and closer to Sodom. Abram is living by faith and will be greatly blessed. Lot is living in the "way which seems right to a man" (Proverbs 14:12) and will lose it all.

We have covered a lot of territory as we have walked through Genesis 12-13 in this lesson. Day by day, we have seen Abram's heart being transformed. More and more, he is thinking God-thoughts and acting in God-ways. Now is a good time to pause and think about your own faith journey.

6. How has God spoken to you through His Word this week?

7. 1 John 5:4 tells us, "For whatever is born of God overcomes the world; and this is the victory that has overcome the world – our faith." What does that promise from God mean to you?

If you believe in a God who controls the big things, you have to believe in a God who controls the little things. It is we, of course, to whom things look "little" or "big." [37]

~ Elisabeth Elliot

day five

Blessed to Be a Blessing

And I will make you a great nation, And I will bless you,
And make your name great; And so you shall be a blessing.
Genesis 12:2

Blessed be the God and Father of our Lord Jesus Christ, who has blessed
us with every spiritual blessing in the heavenly places in Christ.
Ephesians 1:3

In our lesson this week, we saw that when God establishes a people for Himself through His covenant with Abram, He makes this promise: "And I will make you a great nation, And I will bless you, And make your name great; And so you shall be a blessing; And I will bless those who bless you, And the one who curses you I will curse. And in you all the families of the earth will be blessed" (Genesis 12:2-3). God's heart has always been fixed upon blessing His people; it is His default setting.

In fact, the theme of blessing shapes the entire narrative of Scripture. The very first thing God does after He creates Adam and Eve is to bless them (Genesis 1:27-28). Before there was original sin, there was original blessing. Let that sink in. The blessing of God then weaves its way from Eden to Mesopotamia where God forms a people for Himself by blessing Abram and promising to bless the nations through him (Genesis 12:1-3). Subsequently, the stories of Abram's descendants, Isaac, Jacob, Esau, and Joseph, revolve around blessing and the power to bless (Genesis 25:11; 26:3-5; 32:26-30; 35:9; 49:1-27). When the Israelites are wandering in the wilderness, the priests follow God's instructions to Moses and regularly pronounce a blessing over the people (Numbers 6:22-23). God then expounds on the blessing at Mount Gerizim (Deuteronomy 28:1-14). After David brings the Ark of the Lord back to Jerusalem, he returns home to bless his family (1 Chronicles 16:43). The first words in the Old Testament hymnal are "Blessed is the man..." (Psalm 1:1). Then in the New Testament after Jesus is born and His parents take Him to the temple to consecrate Him to the Lord, Simeon blesses Him and His family (Luke 2:22-35). Years later, Jesus begins His earthly ministry with a series of blessings called the Beatitudes (Matthew 5:1-12). And the very last thing that Jesus does before His ascension is to bless the disciples (Luke 24:51). Then, in the final chapter of Revelation, the last blessing in Scripture is the eternal blessing, "Blessed are those who wash their robes, so that they may have the right to the tree of life, and may enter by the gates into the city" (Revelation 22:14).

Blessing is a foundational teaching of Scripture. While believers today are under the new covenant and cannot claim the old covenant blessings promised to Abram in the same way, Wiersbe reminds us that "the principle of 'faith and obedience bring blessing' still applies even though the promised blessings may be different." [38] He continues:

> The just still live by faith, and faith still leads to obedience, and obedience leads to God's blessing (Hebrews 10:38-39, James 2:14-26). We obey because we love Him, not because we want rewards; and that loving obedience of faith opens the door for the Lord to bless us and make us a blessing. Hebrews 11 proves that God has always honored the faith and obedience of those who trust and obey. [39]

1. Read Galatians 3:13-14. How has the blessing of Abraham come to us?

For those who place their faith in Christ, God has already "blessed us with every spiritual blessing in the heavenly places in Christ" (Ephesians 1:3). By faith, we can draw from His unlimited riches. We are blessed! And we are blessed to be a blessing to others.

The Hebrew word for blessing, *baruch,* is used over 600 times in the Old Testament and means "good word." [40] We all crave the blessing, don't we? We long to hear a good word, an affirmation. And when we give a blessing to someone, "we are speaking 'good words' of truth about how God sees them and loves them." [41]

To help us to grasp the significance of blessing, Alan Wright poses this question, "Has anyone ever looked you in the eye, affirmed your infinite value, identified your unique gifts, and pointed you toward a God-given destiny?" [42]

2. What would it mean to you for someone to give a blessing like that over your life?

3. How do you think your loved ones would respond to you speaking "good words" over them?

Blessed to Be a Blessing

In February 2013 as Dallas Willard's life on earth was drawing to an end, he spoke at a conference in Santa Barbara, California, on spiritual formation and life in the Kingdom. His final session in the conference was simply titled, *Blessing*. He shared the following words,

> As followers of Christ, we want to be points of constant blessing moving out to everyone around us....Blessing is the projection of good into the life of another. It isn't just words. It's the actual putting forth of your will for the good of another person. It always involves God, because when you will the good of another person, you realize only God is capable of bringing that....This is the nature of blessing. It is what we are to receive from God and then give to another....It's a generous outpouring of our whole being into blessing the other person....Imagine now becoming a person of blessing; imagine you and others being characterized by the blessing flowing out from you. Our communities would be spotted with points of light from whom blessing flows. The church then would become an overwhelming presence in the community, and the love that flows in the community would become the testimony of the reality of Jesus and of God's plan and of the Kingdom at work in us. [43]

Blessed people bless people.

Willard's challenge to become a "person of blessing" will be our weekly focus for Day Five throughout our study. Blessed people bless people. Learning about the blessing is good, but we want to move from learning to living. *It's time to go all in and all out for the All in All.* Let's determine to be a "person of blessing" and see "the Kingdom at work in us."

Every day, we have untold opportunities to bless others with our words and our practical deeds. This week, keep a "Blessed to Be a Blessing" list going of the occasions God gives you to bless others.

"Blessed to Be a Blessing" list:

_____   _____

_____   _____

_____   _____

_____   _____

ABRAM BELIEVES
Genesis 14-15

The issue of faith is not so much whether we believe in God,
but whether we believe the God we believe in. [1]
~ R.C. Sproul

Abram has been called by God and is following and obeying His voice. As we saw in the last lesson, just like you and me, he does not do it perfectly. But as we journey along with him, we are going to witness his faith grow exponentially.

The Background. After the trip to Egypt, Abram is back in the land of Canaan with his nephew Lot. They returned from Egypt with such a great number of livestock and servants that they were no longer able to remain together in the same area. Abram gave Lot his choice of the land. And Lot selected what appeared to him as the best real estate, the well-watered valley of the Jordan. We are going to see that things are not always as they appear.

Lot chose the land that looked most desirable to the natural man. The enemy quite often disguises the things of this world with affluence and ease. Only the person who walks by faith is able to discern the wise and God-honoring choice. And as we will discover, our choices have very definite consequences, not just for us, but for our descendants as well.

Genesis 14:1-16

Genesis 14 has all the makings of a great war movie, with lots of action and a surprising twist at the end. This passage records the first battle in the Bible, and it is not just a border skirmish. This is a full-blown battle with nations and kings fighting for dominance. Alliances have been formed. The five kings of the valley are rebelling against the four kings who have made them subject to their rule and have exacted tribute (taxes) from them for twelve years.

Read Genesis 14:1-9.

1. In the chart below, identify the kings who are battling against each other (vv. 1-2).

The Four Kings	The Five Kings
1. Amraphel, king of Shinar	1. Bera, king of Sodom
2.	2.
3.	3.
4.	4.
	5.

Years before Abram had entered Canaan, Chedorlaomer, a Napoleon-type conqueror of the day, had subdued the towns in the Jordan Valley. No one could access the road between Damascus and Memphis without paying a tax. In the thirteenth year, the men of Sodom, Gomorrah, Admah, Zeboiim, and Bela have grown weary of Chedorlaomer's domination and have decided to form a coalition to stage a revolt. F.B. Meyer details what Chedorlaomer does to chastise their rebellion and regain his upper hand:

> Combining his own forces with those of the three vassal and friendly rulers in the Euphrates Valley, which lay in his way, he swept across the desert and fell upon the wild tribes that harbored in the mountains of Bashan and Moab. His plan was evidently to ravage the whole country contiguous to those Jordan towns before actually invading them. At last the allied forces concentrated in the neighborhood of Sodom, where they encountered fierce resistance. [2]

Read Genesis 14:10-16.

2. Where do the kings line up to face each other in the battle? (v. 10)

Verse 10 tells us the valley was full of "tar pits." One commentator referenced the pits in the valley: "Notice the indication of the future judgment given in the course of the narrative – 'the valley of Siddim was full of slime-pits.' God's vengeance underlies the wicked, ready to burst forth on them in due time." [3] These pits, which many believe to be volcanic in nature, could very easily have been what erupted raining fire and brimstone on Sodom and Gomorrah in Genesis 19.

We might think that the five kings fighting on their own turf would easily be able to defeat the four invading kings, but that is not what happens.

3. What happens to the five kings and their armies? (v. 10)

In the midst of the battle, Lot and his family are captured and become prisoners of war.

4. Where is Lot living when he and his family are taken captive? (vv. 11-12)

Lot had looked at Sodom, moved toward Sodom (Genesis 13:10-13), and now he is living in Sodom. Warren Wiersbe explains that Lot's capture is "God's way of disciplining him and reminding him that he has no business living in Sodom." [4]

Up until this time, Abram has not been involved in the war. But that all changes when he finds out that his nephew has been captured when Sodom was overrun.

5. What does Abram do when he hears that Lot is taken captive? (v. 14)

Abram could have easily thought that Lot was getting what he deserved. After all, he had chosen the best of the land for himself. He had gotten himself into this mess. But we don't see this attitude in Abram. His compassion and responsibility lead him to risk his own life for his wayward nephew.

6. How many trained men does Abram take with him? (v. 14)

These men are like Abram's personal Delta Force. He has trained them, and they are prepared for battle.

7. How does Abram defeat the enemy kings? (vv. 14-15)

Abram, his trained men, and his allies (Mamre, Eschol, and Aner) are so strong that they chase the enemy north of Damascus (about a hundred miles) and rescue Lot and his family. But in the end, he doesn't just rescue his nephew. Abram frees all of the captives and recovers a massive amount of plunder from the enemy.

As we wrap up today's lesson, let me leave you with two important principles we can learn from this episode in Abram and Lot's lives:

> **Beware of compromise.** Leaning into the world and its value system only leads to sin and suffering. Just ask Lot. If he had not been in Sodom in the first place, he would not have needed to be rescued.

> **Be prepared for the battle.** Abram had his men ready for battle. His example models Ephesians 6:10-11 for us, "Finally, be strong in the Lord and in the strength of His might. Put on the full armor of God, so that you will be able to stand firm against the schemes of the devil." When the enemy attacks you, and he will, are you spiritually prepared?

day two

Genesis 14:17-24

As we move into the second half of Genesis 14, one battle is over, but another one is about to commence. Only this time, the battle is spiritual.

Abram believes God and is walking by faith. Consequently, he has a different perspective than those who walk by sight. As Abram and those with him approach the Dead Sea on their return home, two kings come out to meet him – the King of Salem and the King of Sodom. Abram's faith will continue to guide him and grant him wisdom as he encounters these two vastly different kings.

Read Genesis 14:17-20.

1. Who is the first king that meets Abram? (v. 17)

Bera, the king of Sodom, rules over the most perverse and morally corrupt city in all of the ancient world. For some reason, he has escaped and galloped off to freedom while all of his citizens have been taken as prisoners of war. Then comes an astonishing twist in this story.

2. Who is the second king that greets Abram? (v. 18)

3. How is Melchizedek described? (v. 18)

In Hebrew, the name Melchizedek means "king of righteousness" and Salem means "peace." He is the king of righteousness and peace! [5] And then Moses tells us that this mysterious king is a priest of God Most High. That detail is surprising for one simple reason – Old Testament priests did not yet exist. The priesthood would not be established until the time of Moses 600 years later.

4. What name is used for God in verses 18-20?

El Elyon, God Most High, refers to God as the one true God, the God above all other gods, the Lord and Ruler of the universe, the "Possessor" or Creator of Heaven and earth. This description differentiates God from the polytheistic pagan gods who themselves were created. When Melchizedek greets Abram, he does two things. First, he blesses him in the name of the Lord. Then, he reminds him that God is the One Who delivered his enemies into his hand.

Before we continue, let's press the pause button on Melchizedek. Just who is this man? First, who he is not – Melchizedek is not a Jew. At this time, Abram and Sarai are the only Jews. And since the priesthood does not yet exist, his appointment has not come from the Law; it has come from God. Here is the significance we need to see. God is setting up the foundation for His redemptive plan that will ultimately be fulfilled through His Son, Jesus. Like Melchizedek, Jesus was not a descendant of Levi (the tribe of the priests), but chosen by God and a descendant of Judah. Hebrews 7:22 tells us that "Jesus has become the guarantee of a better covenant." In other words, He fulfilled the Old Testament Law and ushered in a new covenant. In the new covenant, Jesus is the sole legitimate High Priest.

5. Read Hebrews 6:20. What description does the writer give to Jesus?

6. Read Hebrews 7 for the New Testament account of Abram's meeting with Melchizedek. What does the writer tell us about the priesthood of Christ? (vv. 23-28)

The writer of Hebrews makes it clear that the priesthood of Christ is superior to the old Levitical order and the priesthood of Aaron.

7. What assurance does the writer give to those who are in Christ? (v. 25)

Now back to our question. Who is this Melchizedek? Some commentators believe that he is a pre-incarnate appearance of Jesus Christ, referencing Hebrews 7:3 which says Melchizedek was "without father, without mother, without genealogy, having neither beginning of days nor end of life, but made like the Son of God, he remains a priest perpetually." At the very least, we know that he is a "type" of Christ, pointing to His future coming as Savior, Redeemer, Prophet, Priest, and King.

8. What does Abram give to Melchizedek? (Genesis 14:20; Hebrews 7:4)

Read Genesis 14:21-24.

9. What does the king of Sodom offer to Abram? (v. 21)

10. What is Abram's response and why? (vv. 22-24)

One scholar makes this observation about Abram's answer to Bera, king of Sodom:

> Abram's strict separation from the worldly power, which he rested on an oath of faithfulness to God, shows that he is decidedly advancing in spiritual character. The contrast is very striking between his conduct and that of Lot. He at the same time does not attempt to enforce his own high principle upon others. The Church of God has suffered much from its attempts to apply its own high rules to the world instead of leaving the world to find out for itself their superiority and adopt them. [6]

Let me share a couple of final thoughts with you:

A test often follows a great victory. The king of Sodom approached Abram after the victory had been won, not before. What happened with Abram can happen to us. After you have seen an answer to prayer, experienced victory in an area of your life, or passed an important spiritual test, the enemy will often come after you. So be aware!

As we mature spiritually, we will continue to be tempted by the things of the world. As the king of Sodom dangled the treasures of the world in front of Abram, he had to decide if God was enough. When that happens to you –

> Turn your eyes upon Jesus
> Look full in His wonderful face
> And the things of earth will grow strangely dim
> In the light of His glory and grace. [7]

day three

Genesis 15:1-7

During the Boxer Rebellion at the turn of the 20th century, the China Inland Mission lost 58 missionaries and 21 of their children. Many of them were beheaded. Two single female missionaries were executed as they were kneeling to pray. As he was agonizing over the severity of the situation, the founder of the mission, Hudson Taylor, summarized his spiritual situation, "I cannot read. I cannot think. I cannot even pray. But I can trust." [8] During this desperate time, Taylor struggled. While it is unlikely that any of us have walked through that depth of despair, we have all been through hard times. Times when our fears and doubts are winning the day. Times when we could echo the words of Hudson Taylor.

That is where we find Abram at the beginning of Genesis 15.

Read Genesis 15:1-6.

Abram was called by God to leave his family and land to travel to a place that God would show him. As he has stepped out in obedience, we have seen Abram grow in his faith and dependence upon God. In Genesis 12:2, God had promised him descendants through whom the "families of the earth would be blessed." But that has yet to happen. And at the beginning of Genesis 15, Abram is struggling with doubt and fear. Imagine the questions that are probably running through Abram's mind: How much longer will we have to wait for a child? Why is Sarai still barren? Is God punishing us for some sin? Has God forgotten us? Is there a Plan B?

From a human point of view, Abram's doubts seem reasonable, don't they? He is now getting close to 85, and several years have passed since God had given him the promise. And besides that, Sarai is also struggling with her own set of doubts. If you really think about it, the only reason that Abram has to keep on believing is that God said so. Will God's promise to him be enough to sustain him?

1. When God speaks to Abram in a vision, how does He reassure him? (v. 1)

2. Think back on what has just occurred in Genesis 14. Why might God's promise to be his "shield" and his "great reward" speak directly to Abram?

Note that God does not tell Abram that He will give him a shield. He tells him that He will be his shield. God's shield is undefeatable. It is as strong as God is!

3. After Abram questions God, what does God do and say in response? (vv. 4-5)

What a staggering visual! Millions of twinkling stars are spread before Abram. God is telling him that although no offspring is yet in sight, millions are on the way. From this point forward, regardless of if Abram looks down at the dust (Genesis 13:14) or up at the sky, he will be reminded that he can believe what God has promised will come to pass.

4. Genesis 15:6 is the salvation verse of the Old Testament. What does Abram do to be counted righteous?

As God speaks, Abram believes. Wiersbe reminds us that "promises do us no good unless we believe them and act upon them." [9] Salvation does not depend upon us, but upon what Christ has done for us. Salvation has always been by grace through faith.

5. Read James 2:21-24. In this passage, James quotes Genesis 15:6. What does he say about Abraham's faith?

It is biblically clear that we are saved by grace through faith and not of works (Ephesians 2:8-9). But it is also abundantly clear in Scripture that saving faith produces works. Real faith is a faith that works. Once we believe, we will obey.

Real faith is a faith that works.

6. How do you see your faith impacting the work to which God has called you?

Like Abram, we will go through times when we question God. Like Hudson Taylor, there will be times when we will struggle to read our Bibles, to pray, to focus our thoughts on God. But when we can do nothing else, we can still trust His loving hand. Dear friend, stay the course. Believe God. Stand on His promises. Just like His eye is on the sparrow, He is watching over you.

day four

Genesis 15:7-21

What happens next will seem very strange to us. However, in Abram's culture, the "Covenant Ceremony" was a recognizable and familiar ceremony used to formalize transactions between two parties. In those days, you did not sign a contract. Instead, you would cut an animal and walk between the parts, saying, "May I be cut off or destroyed if I do not uphold this covenant." Once you participated, you were bound by the curse if you failed to uphold the covenant. Abram understands the covenant process, but it will not go as Abram has anticipated.

Read Genesis 15:7-11.

1. How does God describe Himself to Abram at the opening of the covenant? (v. 7)

This initial phrase in the Abrahamic covenant is important to note because God will use an identical format when He introduces the Mosiac covenant in Exodus 20:2, "I am the Lord your God, who brought you out of the land of Egypt, out of the house of slavery." Kent Hughes makes this observation:

> Thus, the two most formative events in the history of the Jewish people – Abram's exodus from Ur and Moses' exodus from Egypt – were prefaced with identical language. Also, both the Abrahamic covenant and the Mosaic covenant were based on sovereign acts of salvation: first in Abram's deliverance from Ur and then in Moses' deliverance from Egypt. [10]

When Abram asks how he can know that he will possess the land, it is a question from a believing heart. God answers Abram by making a covenant with him.

2. What instructions does God give to Abram? (v. 9)

After he obediently gathers the animals, Abram divides all of them, except for the birds, in two, and lays the halves out like two sides of an aisle.

Read Genesis 15:12-21.

The preparations obviously take him all day because it is now nighttime. God causes a deep sleep to come upon Abram as He allows him to "see" how the future history will unfold for his descendants, the Jewish people. The Lord reveals that Abram's descendants will be in a foreign land (Egypt) for 400 years, but that He will deliver them from their oppression, and they will come out with many possessions.

3. What does God tell Abram about his death? (v. 15)

This assurance will alleviate any concerns that Abram might have regarding a retaliation from the four kings he defeated when he was rescuing Lot.

Then something spectacular happens.

4. How does God appear as He passes between the animal parts? (v. 17)

When God reveals Himself as a smoking pot and a blazing torch, it is a theophany, a visible representation of God. God will appear to the Israelites in similar forms, "the pillar of fire" (Exodus 13:21-22) and "smoke" on Mount Sinai (Exodus 19:18), as He guides them toward Canaan centuries later. Thus, we know that it is the Presence of God that passes between the pieces. And while normally, both parties would pass through the walkway, in this instance, only God passes through. Chuck Swindoll writes, "As an act of pure grace, God walked the sacrificial pathway, obligating Himself to fulfill His unconditional covenant with [Abram]." [11]

I recently listened to Tim Keller preach a tremendous lesson on this passage. He points out that this covenant ceremony is a beautiful presentation of the gospel in the Old Testament:

> This was a covenant ratification ceremony…. This is the gospel. This is the whole gospel…
> God appears, and He passes between the pieces. He is saying, "I have promised to bless
> you, Abraham. I have promised to be your God and to bring salvation to the world. I have
> promised and if I do not do what I say, may My immutability experience mutation. May My

immortality suffer mortality, may My infinity suffer limitation and finitude, may My power suffer powerlessness, may the impossible become possible, may I be cut off, may I be destroyed, may My body be ripped to pieces...." God walked through the pieces alone. He did not say Abraham, "Now you do it..." God is saying, "Abraham, I am going through for both of us." Salvation and Christian faith is not a cooperative effort...God says, "I will take upon Myself the curse of the covenant for both of us...may I be cut off if I don't do My part, but Abraham may I be cut off if you don't do yours...." Centuries later, darkness came down again (Mark 15:33)...God was cut off, God was trampled into the dust, the darkness came down upon Him. [12]

What an experience Abram has with God! First, under the vast starry sky, Abram believes that he will have innumerable descendants, and then, God credits that belief to him as righteousness. Following that, in faith, he believes that the land God has promised will one day belong to His people. The darkness flees. The light shines in on his soul. His doubts and fears disappear. God's fiery presence lifts, and Abram wakes up.

Now, more than 4000 years have passed. So, what does this mean to us? Iain Duguid answers that question for us:

> By what figure could God have demonstrated His commitment more graphically to Abram? How could it have been displayed more vividly? The only way would have been for the figure to become a reality, for the ever-living God to take on human nature and taste death in the place of the covenant-breaking children of Abram. And that is precisely what God did in Jesus Christ. On the cross, the covenant curse fell completely on Jesus, so that the guilty ones who place their trust in Him might experience the blessings of the covenant. Jesus bore the punishment for our sins, so that God might be our God and we might be His people. [13]

O, what a Savior we have!

As we wrap up today's lesson, spend some time reflecting on Isaiah 53:6-8:

> *All of us like sheep have gone astray,*
> *Each of us has turned to his own way;*
> *But the Lord has caused the iniquity of us all*
> *To fall on Him.*
> *He was oppressed and He was afflicted,*
> *Yet He did not open His mouth;*
> *Like a lamb that is led to slaughter,*
> *And like a sheep that is silent before its shearers,*

So He did not open His mouth.

By oppression and judgment He was taken away;

And as for His generation, who considered

That He was cut off out of the land of the living

For the transgression of my people, to whom the stroke was due?

Then pause and thank the Lord for all that He has done for us in Christ.

day five

The Blessing of Faith

*By faith Abraham, when he was called, obeyed by going out to a place which
he was to receive for an inheritance; and he went out, not knowing where he was
going. By faith he lived as an alien in the land of promise as in a foreign land,
dwelling in tents with Isaac and Jacob, fellow heirs of the same promise;
for he was looking for the city which has foundations,
whose architect and builder is God.*
Hebrews 11:8-10

We are to follow Abram's example and believe God. Believing is our job (John 6:29). That's why we are called "believers"!

1. Read Hebrews 11:8-10. In what ways can you live in the present as a citizen in the city whose Architect and Builder is the Lord?

In this lesson, we read about God "cutting" a covenant with Abram and his descendants. God committed Himself to uphold the covenant and to be the One Who died if the covenant was broken. This is a beautiful foreshadowing of Christ, who would bear our penalty when He shed His blood for us on Calvary. Jesus was forsaken by God so that we would never be God-forsaken.

Jesus was forsaken by God so that we would never be God-forsaken.

2. Read Psalm 22:1-18. List the passages that are a direct reference to Christ's death on the cross.

Jesus died of thirst, loss of blood, and trauma. He bore the wrath of God in His body on the cross.

When Jesus came to the end of His ministry on earth, He spent His final evening with His disciples. He instituted the Lord's Supper with them, and then taught them as recorded in John 13-17. He closed His time with them in prayer.

3. Read John 17:20-26. What did Jesus pray for us?

Jesus prayed for us to experience the "oneness of essence" that He had with the Father. He prayed for us the very thing that He was about to forfeit for Himself on the cross. Jesus quoted Psalm 22:1, "My God, My God, why have You forsaken Me?" He was forsaken by God, separated from the Father for the first time in all of eternity, that we might be one with the Father.

The Old Covenant was instituted by God and marked by the blood of animals. The New Covenant was instituted by God and marked by the blood of Christ. The Old Covenant led to death under the law, but the New Covenant leads to life in Christ. And not just eternal life, but life abundant, full, overflowing, and free!

Oh, what a Savior! How can we ever praise Him enough for all He has done for us? The eternal justice of God came down on Jesus. The favor and the face of God is what we need. To have it removed would cause our death. In the words of Keller, "He had the ultimate spiritual thirst and died in torment that we might have the cool water of the favor of God." [14]

Jesus was crucified outside the city gate that we might be invited in. Jesus was thirsty, that we might have rivers of living water flowing forth from our inner man. Jesus was stripped, that we might be clothed in His righteousness. Jesus was forsaken, that we might be accepted. Jesus died that we might live forever. Oh, dear friend, BELIEVE!

Blessed to Be a Blessing

In the late 1960's, the Christian musical, "Good News" was written and presented in churches across the world. The seminal song in the musical was titled, "Do You Really Care?" Let me share the lyrics with you:

> I look around in the place that I live
> I see people with so much to give
> Yet there are those who are dying to know
> Just that somebody cares

Do you really care?

Do you know how to share

With people everywhere?

Do you really care?

I see people just longing to know

What they can live for and where they can go

We have the hope, and the purpose to share

But do we really care?

Do you really care?

Do you know how to share

With people everywhere?

Do you really care?

Will you take the dare?

Spread good news everywhere?

The cross of Christ to bear?

Do you really care? [15]

Decades have passed since that song gripped the hearts of those singing it, as well as those who were listening in the pew. But the message still grips my heart. Do we really care about those...

- Who don't look like us?

- Who don't think like us?

- Who don't act like us?

- Who are hurting?

- Who do not know Christ?

Believing friend, if we don't care about them, who will?

As we are focusing on becoming "a person of blessing" in this study, your assignment this week is to bless a stranger. Do something kind for someone you do not know. And when you do, ask if you can pray for the person you blessed. If God opens the door, share the gospel with him or her.

When we think of all that Jesus has done for us, how can we not be moved to share the "Hope" that is within us?

ABRAM IS RENAMED
Genesis 16-18

I am who I am because the I AM tells me who I am. [1]
~ Charity Gayle

The Bible, from beginning to end, is God's love letter to humanity. As His children, He whispers blessings to us throughout this letter and speaks love over us by calling us as He sees us. Who does Jesus say you are?

Christ says you are justified and redeemed (Romans 3:24). But I would venture to say that most days, you don't feel justified or redeemed, because in this present world, Satan attacks our sense of security and hope.

Christ says you are accepted (Romans 15:7). But we spend a lot of time dwelling on the fear and pain of rejection because this world tells us we can never measure up.

Christ says you are a new creature (2 Corinthians 5:17). But if we are honest, there are moments when we feel like we haven't matured in Christ at all, because Satan loves to celebrate our setbacks.

And the list goes on. The good news is that we can believe what Jesus says about us because He sees more than we see. He calls us by names that represent who we will be when we are made perfect in Him.

At this point in their story, Abram and Sarai find themselves stuck between what Paul David Tripp calls the "already" and the "not yet." [2] They have already received a promise from God for a son, but there is no sign of any offspring…yet. As they begin to lose hope, God steps in and reminds them of the promise. He does so by giving them new names – names that, in His eyes, represent the "already" and the "assurance of things hoped for, the conviction of things not seen" (Hebrews 11:1).

This week, we will see the promise of God begin to unfold as both Abram and Sarai are given new names – names that reflect the assurance of God's plan. A plan that can only be accomplished by *El Shaddai*, God Almighty.

If you belong to Christ, you are redeemed, restored, rescued, clean, righteous, loved, adored, and you are white as snow. You are not who you say you are, who the enemy says you are, or who this world says you are.

You are who the I AM says you are.

day one

Genesis 16:1-15

Let's begin today's lesson with a quick reflection from last week. Remember, we are looking toward a promise that has been given to Abram by God Himself. A blessing to assure Abram that his family line will continue beyond what he can imagine.

1. Look back at Genesis 15. How many times do you see the phrase "your descendants"?

God does not do or say anything unintentionally. His repetition here is for a reason. He is driving home some assurance that will be needed as the biological clock continues to tick for Abram and Sarai… but what is a biological clock to the Author of biology?

What is a biological clock to the Author of biology?

Read Genesis 16:1-2.

Today's passage records a detour in Abram and Sarai's walk with the Lord. As Sarai grows impatient waiting, she takes matters into her own hands. As we get ready to walk through this chapter in their story, there is an important note to make here about what we are seeing in Scripture, especially as we digest the fact that "all Scripture is inspired by God" (2 Timothy 3:16).

Tara-Leigh Cobble gives us insight into the ancient world:

> In those days, servants were considered possessions. This is one of those things in Scripture that is *de*scriptive, not *pre*scriptive. It's telling us what **does** happen, not what **should** happen. This is not condoning treating people like possessions. But in that ancient culture, that's what was happening. And anything a servant owned; the master owned. So, a child of a servant was considered property of the master. [3]

Remember, at this point in time, Abram has already received the promise of a son. But ten years have passed since that promise was given. Without a doubt, this is something Abram and Sarai have discussed many times. However, "human impatience drives them to adopt a cultural pattern common at their time and in their part of the world." [4]

2. Look again at the end of verse 2. What does Abram do to consent to this idea?

It's been said before that while the man is the head of the household, the woman is the neck, turning the head wherever she pleases. We say this tongue-in-cheek, but we certainly see at very pivotal points in Scripture how much a woman can influence a man, for better or worse!

As this plan begins to unfold, it goes awry from the beginning.

Read Genesis 16:3-6.

3. Why do you think Hagar despises Sarai after she conceives? (vv. 5-6)

4. What emotions are stirred in Sarai as a result of this conflict? (vv. 5-6)

This section of the story is a bit of a head-scratcher for me. I mean, wasn't all of this Sarai's idea? Does she really have a right to be angry? One scholar sheds some light on this in a way that I think many of us can relate to:

> From Sarai's perspective, a terrible thing happened – Abram succeeded in making Hagar pregnant. This proved beyond all doubt the failure to provide a son to Abram was the fault of Sarai, not her husband. In a culture that so highly valued childbearing, mothering the child of a wealthy and influential man like Abram gave a servant girl like Hagar greater status, and made her appear more blessed than Sarai. [5]

Most of us can't begin to understand the depth of sorrow Sarai has to feel. But we have all felt the pain and insecurity of feeling not good enough. We've been rejected for a job we wanted. We've gone through a breakup. We've been ignored by our husbands. We've watched other women bear children while we remain childless. And our greatest fear is that it's our fault. Now imagine that fear being 100% confirmed before your very eyes. For your husband's greatest joy to be realized through the womb of another woman.

5. In what ways can you empathize with the emotions Sarai is experiencing?

Now that you have grieved with Sarai, the scene shifts to Hagar.

Read Genesis 16:7-15.

6. After Hagar flees, Who finds her sitting alone in the wilderness? (v. 7)

Anytime we see the phrase, "the angel of the Lord", in the Old Testament, it should cause us to pause. This is not "an" angel of the Lord. It is "the" angel of the Lord. Many scholars agree that this could be a pre-incarnate appearance of the Son of God. [6]

What struck me as I read about Hagar is that, by all modern standards, what we are seeing here is the first single mom in Scripture. Isn't that something? A Christophany coupled with the first single mom in Scripture. I believe that Jesus looked down and saw Hagar, and that same heart of compassion He is known for in the New Testament surged within Him and compelled Him to go to her.

7. What promise does God give to Hagar? (vv. 10-12)

Here we see a promise within a promise. Not only is she assured that she will have many descendants, but the very name of her first offspring is God's way of revealing His character. We cannot overestimate what it must have meant to a servant girl from Egypt, who is pregnant and alone, to be told to name her son Ishmael, "God hears." John MacArthur provides us insight, "With her son's name meaning 'God hears,' Hagar the servant could not ever forget how God had heard her cry of affliction." [7]

8. How does Hagar describe the Lord in verse 13?

Hagar meets God in the place she least expects – in the barrenness of the wilderness. Consider the significance of what happens there:

> Hagar encountered God in the desert and addressed Him as *El Roi*, "the God who sees me." Notably, this is the only occurrence of *El Roi* in the Bible. Hagar's God is the One who numbers the hairs on our heads and who knows our circumstances, past, present, and future. When you pray to El Roi, you are praying to the one who knows everything about you. [8]

9. What does it mean to you to know that God sees you?

Anna Harris shares about the importance of Hagar's encounter with God:

> Hagar, a soon to be single mom became the first person in the Bible to name God…What does it mean that Hagar was "seen" by God? To be seen is to be valued, accounted for, and respected as an individual who bears the image of her Creator. Hagar had never truly been seen by another person. Her enslavers saw her as the spoils of conflict. Abram and Sarai saw her as an incubator for the promised child. But God saw her, heard her, and knew her. He understood her history and spoke directly to her greatest fears by providing for her needs and giving her a hopeful future. [9]

Life does not always – in fact it usually does not – pan out the way we hoped. Many days, like Sarai, we feel like failures and scramble to clean up our mess. Some days, like Hagar, we feel overlooked and slink away to the shadows where it feels safer.

But every day, you are walking under the watchful eye of *El Roi* – the God who sees. And His heart of compassion is stirring for you – He will come to your aid.

day two

Genesis 17:1-27

In today's reading, we see one of the most pivotal snapshots in the lives of Abram and Sarai. A blessing and a covenant are bestowed on them that will reverberate throughout the rest of history.

Read Genesis 17:1-8.

1. How many years has it been since Ishmael was born? (Genesis 16:16; 17:1)

Stop for a moment and think about where you were and what you were doing around this time 13 years ago. A lot can happen in that amount of time. Some of you have had major life events take place. You have seen babies born, loved ones pass, graduations, weddings, job changes. The list goes on. Thirteen years may seem like a small amount of time, especially when we flip one page of Scripture and jump more than a decade in Abram's life. But when we insert ourselves into this story, we realize how much life has been lived.

2. How do you think Abram is feeling about the covenant God established with him all those years ago?

3. How does God identify Himself when He begins speaking to Abram in this passage? (v. 1)

Here we see God reveal a name that is more than just a nice character attribute. *El Shaddai*, God Almighty, gives Abram a moment of reassurance.

4. At this point in Abram's life, why does it matter to him that God is Almighty?

When you receive a promise from God, and this can take many forms, there is a spark of hope in your soul about what is to come. Perhaps you have sensed that God is leading you toward a career change, a ministry opportunity, freedom from a long-time stronghold, healing of a relationship – it could be any number of things where you just know in your soul that God is going to move. And then He doesn't. You find yourself living in the "not yet." And that hope can begin to dwindle.

5. Describe a time in your life when you began to grow impatient with the promises of God.

I love that God opens this moment with Abram by giving him, what is in my mind, a booming reassurance, "I AM GOD ALMIGHTY!" This is the kind of reassurance Abram needs for what is coming next.

6. What name does God give Abram in verse 5 and why does He change his name?

God is changing Abram's name to what He knows he will become. Abram means "exalted father," but Abraham means "father of a multitude." He is calling him by the name that is descriptive of his destiny in God's plan. There is absolutely no question in God's mind what will come of Abraham. It is as good as done.

There is something that happens in us when that kind of assurance is spoken over us. Alan Wright says, "When we bless people, we don't tell them what they 'ought' to believe – we tell them the good news that we believe for them." [10]

7. Now skip to Genesis 17:15-22. What new name does Sarai receive? And what promise is Abraham given regarding his wife?

Whatever notion Abraham may have that the promise has already been accomplished through Ishmael is now obliterated by God's words. God's people will come from Abraham's seed – but specifically through the womb of Sarah. A child not yet born.

> This time, God reiterates His covenant promises and speaks a change of identity to both Abram and Sarai....Sarai, whose name meant "my princess," became simply Sarah – princess, a name befitting her role as matriarch of a family who would become as numerous as the stars in the sky. [11]

8. What is Abraham's reaction to this news? (v. 17)

This reaction is quite different from how he has responded to God's other commands and promises. We're not sure if this is laughter of joy or laughter from how far-fetched it must seem for his 90-year-old wife to bear a child. We will see a similar reaction from Sarah when she hears the news – as well as a gentle rebuke from the Lord for this reaction.

Read Genesis 17:9-14.

9. Who all was required to participate in the circumcision? (v. 10)

Max Anders explains that "this was not some new physical sign that God created just for this occasion... God transformed this social custom into an act of religious significance...investing it with new meaning." [12]

Circumcision represented an act of cleansing. This cutting away of the flesh, physically, is one we also see taking place in the New Testament spiritually. God's covenant with Abraham's descendants will reach even to the Gentile nations in the form of spiritual cleansing.

10. Read Colossians 2:9-15. Through Whom are our hearts circumcised? (v. 11)

11. And what is the result of that covenant? (vv. 13-14)

Anders continues,

> So, we have been circumcised as well – new covenant believers whose hearts have been transformed. God has given us a new identity in Jesus Christ…Perhaps the spiritual inclusion of believing Gentiles is implied as early as Genesis 17 when God included people who are not your offspring. [13]

Now read Genesis 17:23-27. Abraham wastes no time in taking this step of obedience. His son and every male in his household are immediately circumcised.

May we take our spiritual circumcision just as seriously and urgently. For those who are separate from Christ, allow Him to perform this spiritual surgery on your heart and your soul. For those who already belong to Christ, allow Him to daily cut away the parts of the flesh that would keep you from experiencing the joy of the covenant.

day three

Genesis 18:1-15

Today's reading is one of my favorites in the life of Abraham. It is both entertaining and powerful, as it culminates in a one-two punch where the character and power of God meet the omniscience of God. But first, let's meet with Abraham in one of his favorite spots.

Read Genesis 18:1.

The oaks (or terebinths) at Mamre appear to be a favorite spot for Abraham:

> This very spot is where Abraham moved when he came back into the Promised Land from Egypt and built an altar there (Genesis 13:18), and apparently stayed there some time (Genesis 14:13). Abraham purchased a field and cave at Mamre, using it for Sarah's burial (Genesis 23:17–19). Abraham himself was buried there (Genesis 25:9), and his son Isaac was buried there (Genesis 49:30, 50:13). [14]

1. Do you have a special place like this where you and God meet together?

On this side of the cross, we have the privilege of meeting with God anywhere. But there is something special about having a designated place where you sit, pray, and just enjoy the presence of God. If you have trouble spending time with God on a daily basis, may I suggest starting with finding your own "spot." Grab your coffee/tea, Bible, and journal, and enjoy your daily appointment with the Lord.

Read Genesis 18:1-2.

2. What does Abraham see when he lifts his eyes? (v. 2)

Peek briefly at Genesis 19:1.

3. Combining the evidence in 18:1-2 and 19:1, who are the three men who visit Abraham?

We are told right out of the gate that *Yahweh* Himself is paying a visit to Abraham, though it does not appear that Abraham knows this yet. He greets these strangers with a common greeting of "Lord," yet still goes out of his way to show them great hospitality.

Anders comments on the connection between Genesis 18 and Hebrews 13:2:

> The first half of Genesis 18 reflects hospitality shown by courtesy and respect. Strangers appeared at the tent. Without giving a second thought to who they might be, Abraham bowed before them, got water for their feet, and offered them rest and a meal. This incident finds its way into the New Testament where we read in Hebrews 13:2, "Do not forget to entertain strangers, for by so doing, some people have entertained angels without knowing it." [15]

Now our focus turns to Sarah, where she finally hears the promise for herself.

Read Genesis 18:9-12.

4. What does Sarah overhear these men telling her husband? (v. 10)

5. What is Sarah's reaction? (v. 12)

I have to sympathize with Sarah here. The woman is 90 years old and overhears strangers saying that within the year, she will have a bouncing baby boy – the one from whom will come Abraham's descendants and a chosen and holy people. All of this, at first, sounds laughable.

6. Who else had this same response? (Genesis 17:17)

Needless to say, Isaac, which means "he laughs," came by his name honestly.

7. In what way does Sarah laugh? (v. 12)

Read Genesis 18:13-15.

Here we see God display two of His most unique attributes: His power and His omniscience.

8. What question does the Lord ask Abraham in response to Sarah's laughter? (v. 14)

Highlight it. Underline it. Star it. Dog-ear it. Write it on the wall. Hang it in your office/kitchen/nursery. Nothing…NOTHING is too difficult for the Lord.

**Nothing…
NOTHING is too
difficult for the Lord.**

As Warren Wiersbe reminds us,

> If you need proof, then listen to Job (42:2), Jeremiah (32:17, 27), the angel Gabriel (Luke 1:37), and the apostle Paul (Ephesians 3:20–21). If God makes a promise, you can be sure He has the power to fulfill it, and He will remain faithful even when we are faithless (2 Timothy 2:13). [16]

9. In what situation in your life do you need this to be true? What are you carrying that feels too difficult for the Lord to handle?

10. If you heard someone say, "By this time next year, that impossible situation will be completely resolved," what do you think your response would be?

Look again at verse 15. For some reason, this makes me smile. Sarah denies her laughter, and God in flesh looks at her, deadpan, "No, but you did laugh." And then we don't hear another word from Sarah until Isaac is born.

Sneak a peek at Genesis 21:5-7.

11. How is Sarah's laughter different this time?

The bottom line of Abraham's life is that, through his lineage, the Savior will one day come. The Messiah, who will crush the head of our enemy, will come from Abraham's descendants, a plan that is set into motion with the life of Isaac.

So, the next time the enemy tells you something is too hard for God, remind him of Abraham, Sarah, and Isaac – and who will get the last laugh.

day four

Genesis 18:16-33

Our passage today takes a hard, unexpected left turn. We go from a blessing to a curse. From the flourishing of one nation to the demise of another. And within one of the darkest moments of Scripture, one that has rippled through the ages, we see one of the boldest conversations between God and man.

Read Genesis 18:16-23.

1. From this passage alone, what do we know about the state of things in Sodom and Gomorrah? (v. 20)

At this point in the story, we don't yet know what is happening in these cities, but we know it's really bad. God lets Abraham know that He will go see for Himself how grave the sin has become.

2. Do you think God already knew the state of things in Sodom and Gomorrah? If so, why does He need to go see the situation?

F.B. Meyer sheds some light:

> God always closely investigates the true condition of the case before He awards or executes His sentences…He walks our streets day and night. He patrols our thoroughfares, marking everything, missing nothing. He glides unasked into our most sacred privacy, for all things are naked and open to the eyes of Him with whom we have to do. He is prepared, nay, eager to give us the benefit of any excuse. But flagrant sin, like that which broke out in Sodom that very night, is enough to settle forever the fate of a Godless community when standing in the court of Him who is Judge and Witness both. [17]

3. Read Abraham's response in verse 23. What is God planning to do to these cities because of their sin?

MacArthur explains, "the iniquity of the two cities, by then complete, had reached the point of no return before the Lord, who demonstrated before Abraham how justly He assessed the time for judgment." [18]

In the verses that follow, we see a very interesting, almost cringe-worthy conversation happening between God and Abraham.

4. Read verses 24-33. How many times does Abraham go back to God to negotiate?

5. What emotions are stirred within you as you read this exchange?

Abraham is standing in the gap for his people. He boldly and humbly approaches the throne of grace (Hebrews 4:16), laying a precedent that we can follow.

> It would be easy to say that this prayer comes near to haggling, but the right word is "exploring": Abraham is feeling his way forward in a spirit of faith (superbly expressed in [Genesis 18:25] where he grasps the range and rightness of God's rule), of humility, in his whole mode of address, and of love, demonstrated in his concern for the whole city, not for his kinsmen alone. [19]

6. Read Ezekiel 22:30-31. In this passage, what is the job of the man who stands in the gap?

7. What is Abraham's method of standing in the gap? (Genesis 18:23-33)

For some reason, God has allowed Abraham to see and understand the wrath that is about to be poured out on the people of Sodom and Gomorrah. And Abraham's immediate response is prayer. He appeals to the character of God – a God who is loving and righteous and just. MacArthur provides this insight:

> That the number of righteous people necessary to forestall judgment had been reduced from 50 to 10 may have reflected Abraham's awareness both of the intense wickedness of the cities as well as Lot's ineffective witness there. Abraham probably had the whole of Lot's family in mind. [20]

Our pastor, Steve Gaines, often says, "There are some things God will do whether we pray or not. But there are some things God will only do when we pray." [21] We don't know if God's mind was changed by Abraham. At the end of the day, it doesn't matter, because – spoiler alert – there are not even ten righteous people in the land. But there is something important established between Abraham and God that day.

8. What do you think it meant to Abraham to know that God listened when he spoke?

God is the same yesterday, today, and forever (Hebrews 13:8), and countless times throughout the Bible, we are told that God wants to hear our requests, He wants us to ask and keep on asking. There is something powerful that happens in the quiet place of prayer. The Lord Almighty bends His ear to listen to what we have to say.

Who currently needs you to stand in the gap for them? Who needs you to boldly approach the throne and pray on their behalf? Does the situation seem hopeless? Abraham is not ignorant of what is happening in Sodom and Gomorrah. He knows what the cities deserve. But regardless of how hopeless the situation has become, he still goes to God. He asks. And he keeps on asking.

Charles Spurgeon writes,

> If they [lost sinners] will not hear you speak, they cannot prevent your praying. Do they jest at your exhortations? They cannot disturb you at your prayers. Are they far away so that you cannot reach them? Your prayers can reach them. Have they declared that they will never listen to you again, nor see your face? Never mind, God has a voice which they must hear. Speak to Him, and He will make them feel. Though they now treat you despitefully, rendering evil for your good, follow them with your prayers. Never let them perish for lack of your supplications. [22]

9. What does Abraham do at the end of the conversation? (v. 33b)

Just like Abraham, we are to cry out to God with our request, and then leave the result in His very capable hands.

day five

The Blessing of a New Name

He who has an ear, let him hear what the Spirit says to the churches. To him who overcomes, to him I will give some of the hidden manna, and I will give him a white stone, and a new name written on the stone which no one knows but he who receives it.
Revelation 2:17

A groundbreaking study by Betty Hart and Todd Risley called "The Early Catastrophe" found that there is power behind the words that we speak to children between birth and the age of four. The study showed that the more we speak encouraging things to a child at an early age, the fewer problems they will have with identity and purpose later in life. There is power behind words, and moreover, the labels that we attach to ourselves. [23]

If prompted, each one of us could quickly call to mind a time, maybe even from our childhood, when someone made us feel small, insignificant, or not good enough. These "curses" are not things we easily forget. But equally memorable is a moment of genuine blessing – when someone takes time to speak words of life over us.

1. To 99-year-old Abram, what do you think it meant to him for His Creator to change his name to Abraham, "father of a multitude of nations" (Genesis 17:5)?

This moment reinforces a promise God had made to Abram that he would one day have a son with Sarai, and God was letting Abram know He would make good on that promise. God wasn't naming him based on who he was – He was naming him on the basis of who he would become. Abram would never forget that moment.

When you and I meet our Savior, Revelation 2:17 says we will be given a new name – a name that is a secret name between only us and Jesus. I try to imagine what that name might be. I don't picture Jesus scrolling through the trending list of popular baby names when He renames us. Will it even be a word I've ever heard before?

God wasn't naming him based on who he was – He was naming him on the basis of who he would become.

I think we can be sure that it's a name we would've never given ourselves. One we would've never been brave enough or confident enough to claim. A name that, in our perfected state, represents how Jesus has always seen us – one that represents the potential and purpose He knew we would fulfill, even when we never believed it could be possible.

As image bearers of God, we have great power to bless those around us in memorable ways. As sons and daughters of Adam, we also have great power to curse others when we are walking in our flesh.

Today, we have an opportunity to choose life (Deuteronomy 30:19), to bring lasting encouragement to those around us by creating a moment of blessing.

2. Why is it so important to bless and encourage others?

3. As God's image bearers, how do we have the ability to breathe new life into someone who is discouraged?

4. How would it affect your day to receive an unexpected word of blessing from someone?

Blessed to Be a Blessing

As we close out this week on the value of a new name, I want to challenge you to think of three women who need the reminder of their place in Christ. Sometimes we just need someone to wrap an arm around our shoulder, lean in, and remind us that we are now "white as snow" (Isaiah 1:18). It is unlikely that is the way we would describe ourselves on any given day. What would it mean to you for someone to remind you of your value in Christ? Your cleanness in Christ? Pray now for God to lay three names on your heart, and before the enemy talks you out of it, reach out to them and tell each one that she is "white as snow."

four

ABRAHAM IS REMEMBERED
Genesis 19-21

*God's message to the lost world is that judgment is coming,
but His promise to His own people is that He will rescue them.* [1]
~ Warren Wiersbe

God's character. It is steady and true. It will never fail nor will it ever contradict what He's done in the past. While we do not always understand His ways, we can always trust His heart.

God knows us and He wants to make Himself known to us. The Hebrew word, *yada,* means "to know" and is used multiple times throughout Scripture. When the term is used to define the relationship between man and God, it speaks of a deep intimacy that the Father longs to have with His children. [2]

While we do not always understand His ways, we can always trust His heart.

In her book, *Waymaker*, Ann Voskamp writes,

> To know this God, you will have to stay close enough to touch Him. Close enough to touch, to trace every word, every line, from His Word, from His lips, to lean the whole weight of your world upon Him and trust how He holds, to turn and caress His bare heart. Then, and only then, after you've touched Him, experienced God, encountered God, do you know God. [3]

The events of Genesis 19 through 21 will weigh heavy on our hearts as we see evil graphically portrayed. Even in the midst of heinous sin, we will see the goodness of God, the mercy of our Savior, and God's divine intervention on behalf of His people. As you study this text, I pray that you come to *yada* the heart of your Father more deeply and intimately than when you began.

day one

Genesis 19:1-29

As Genesis 18 closes, Abraham is pleading with the Lord to spare Sodom if just ten righteous people can be found. Then Genesis 19 opens with two angels coming into the city to warn Lot of the hastening judgment and to offer him a way out. In just the chapter before, they had appeared to Abraham as men, and yet, to Lot they take the form of angels.

John Phillips gives a possible explanation for this change:

> The changed appearance typified that they had appeared to Abraham as men, to Lot they appeared as angels. The changed appearance typified distance; they were not nearly so close or so cordial with Lot as they had been with Abraham. He saw them in their angelic form although to his unsaved cronies they appeared to be men. The sight of an angel would have been too much for them. [4]

Read Genesis 19:1-3.

1. Upon their arrival, where do the two angels find Lot? (v. 1)

2. What does Lot's position at the gate tell us? (v. 1)

Let us look back for a moment at how this journey began. Here we will see where Lot's first love for the world came into play.

3. What do we learn about Lot from Genesis 13:1, 10-13?

Wiersbe says, "Worldliness is not a matter of physical geography but of heart attitude. Lot's heart was in Sodom long before his body arrived there." [5]

Six chapters before, Lot has his sights set on Sodom. The Bible tells us that he "pitched his tents near Sodom" (Genesis 13:12, NIV). Obviously, he is intrigued by the city and determined to live near it. And seemingly, he never got over it…tragically so.

I have a prayer card from years ago that reads, "Lord, may I never satisfy my soul's appetite at the world's table." While there is nothing new under the sun, modern civilization is even more bombarded with the world's "slop" by way of the internet, social media, movies, and television. The devil has no new tactics, but he is crafty as he dangles the shiny things of the world before us. Make no mistake. Sin can be fun and exciting. It can bring great satisfaction and fulfillment. But only for a moment and at much too high a price.

Consider your physical location, the activities in which you participate, the forms of media you consume, and the attitude of your heart toward sin.

4. How can you choose differently from Lot as you "pitch your tent"?

While Lot was hospitable in greeting his guests by insisting they sleep inside for safety and preparing them a feast, he quickly acts in a way that once again reveals the condition of his heart.

Read Genesis 19:4-9.

5. What do the men of Sodom request and how does Lot respond? (vv. 4-8)

This response shows the depth of Lot's depravation and perversion. His heart has absorbed so much of the wicked culture that he will offer his most precious earthly treasures, his virgin daughters. Tony Evans says this action "reveals Lot's moral ties to Sodom as well as his failure to believe that God would protect him." [6]

6. What insight can you gain from these verses as you ponder Lot's choices?

Romans 12:2

James 1:27b

1 John 2:15-17

Before we continue, let's stop and reflect on the unfailing character of God. It is heart-wrenching to consider all that is taking place in Sodom...the depravity, the perversion, the darkness. But praise be to our God! He shows Himself faithful as He offers a rescue plan for Lot and his family. This is a beautiful picture of Romans 5:8, which tells us, "But God demonstrates his own love for us in this: While we were still sinners, Christ died for us" (NIV).

In our muck and mire, He reaches down and offers us His holy hand. He will not force us to take it. He will not make us choose Him. But oh, how He longs that we do! While we were sinners (not after we were cleaned up and presentable), He sent His only Son to die for us.

Read Genesis 19:10-26.

7. What do the angels do as the men try to break down the door? (vv. 10-11)

8. What further provision is made for Lot and his family as the angels question Lot? (vv. 12-13)

Lot warns his family to get out of the city, yet verse 16 tells us that he still hesitates. His heart tie to the world remains strong. Even in his hesitancy, after several warnings, the Lord continues to move on his behalf. The angels literally take his hand (like a defiant toddler) and the hands of his family and rush them to safety.

9. Why do the angels intervene? (v. 16b)

The Lord is merciful and has "compassion" on Lot. Do those words not just grip your heart, stopping you in your tracks as you read this account? How undeserving! How understandable if God had given Lot over to his way and left him there! Not only was Lot rescued from destruction, but his request to go to Zoar was even granted. Mercy. Abundant mercy. This is our God.

**Mercy.
Abundant mercy.
This is our God.**

After Lot and his family are safely out of Sodom, God rains down fire and burning sulfur on Sodom and Gomorrah. It is utterly destroyed, "wiping out all the people and every bit of vegetation" (Genesis 19:25b, NLT). Lot's wife, clinging to the past, looks back. As a result of this unwillingness to turn away completely, she turns into a pillar of salt. While God's mercy abounds, His judgment must still come. We must never confuse His mercy with His staunch view of our sin.

Let us close today's lesson with our eyes fixed on the heart of God.

10. What do we see about the impact of prayer and the character of God in Genesis 19:27-29?

But God.

But where sin abounded, grace abounded much more.
Romans 5:20, NKJV

day two

Genesis 19:30-38

Just when you think the narrative cannot get worse, we have an unsavory sequel to the destruction of Sodom and Gomorrah. Evans accurately states, "When we try to solve God's 'problems' for Him, we only create more problems for ourselves." [7]

When I first read and studied the Bible chronologically, I began to see that man's reasoning repeatedly got man into trouble, and it still does. When we place our human reasoning above that of a perfect and sovereign God, we reap consequences beyond our control and our wildest dreams. As one person I read said, "One step in the wrong direction led to all of this. One choice. Many consequences." [8]

Before we look at the scheme Lot's daughters devise, let's observe the frame of mind in which we find Lot.

1. According to Genesis 19:30, where does Lot go and why?

Disobedience leads to grave consequences. Facing consequences leads to fear. Fear often leads us to run away and hide. Lot's sinful choices result in the absence of joy and freedom. While we do not live under condemnation (Romans 8:1), most, if not all of us, can think back to a time when we walked our own way, followed our reasoning rather than God's, faced the sting of consequences, and just wanted to hide away. "The joy of the Lord is [our] strength" (Nehemiah 8:10), but I would say the opposite is also true. The <u>absence</u> of the joy of the Lord zaps our strength and can send us running to hide in a cave, plagued by weakness and fear.

2. What quandary do Lot's daughters find themselves in and what is their plan to resolve the issue? (vv. 31-36)

Lot's daughters are desperate. They fear they might never marry and bear children, so they stoop to incest, showing their acceptance of the morals of Sodom. As the *Life Application Study Bible* warns us, "We are most likely to sin when we are desperate for what we feel we must have." [9]

Oh, the power of generational sin! If you are a parent or grandparent (or find yourself in a place of influence over the younger generation), your choices matter. Blessing or curse...this is what we bring into the life of those over whom we have influence. No doubt that Lot's choice to move toward Sodom, and then allow the culture to infiltrate his own heart, is what lays the groundwork for his daughters to take sin lightly or dismiss it altogether, particularly sexual sin. Devoted Christian parenting does not guarantee Christ-following children; however, choosing to live a life marked by holiness and Christlikeness will certainly be blessed by God, and greatly increase the chances of those coming behind us to choose the same.

Lot's daughters manipulate him (human reasoning) by getting him drunk and having sexual relations with him while he is unaware of what is taking place. They go to great lengths, sinful extremes, to accomplish what they feel they must have. Sadly, it seems they are following in the footsteps of their father and mother.

3. Who is the son of the older daughter? (v. 37)

4. Who is the son of the younger daughter? (v. 38)

Their descendants, "Moab and Ben-ammi became the fathers of two of Israel's greatest enemies, the Moabites and the Ammonites. These nations settled east of the Jordan River, and Israel never conquered them." [10]

Do you think these young women ever stopped to consider the result of their scheme? Do you think they played out this scenario to what could be? Of course not! That is what the enemy still does to us today. He hurls a fiery dart at our minds, a clever plan that will give us what we want and think we need, yet we often fail to carefully consider the long-term consequences of the choice. We settle for instant gratification rather than seeing the eternal ramification.

These women want children. They do not trust God to take care of them, just as Lot did not trust God to take care of him and his family.

5. What are some ways the enemy lies to you and tempts you to take matters into your own hands rather than trusting the hand of God?

Mark Batterson writes,

> Sin is the epitome of poor judgment. More often than not, sin is meeting a legitimate need in an illegitimate way. Sin is not worth the price we have to pay, and we know that, yet we do it. The question, of course, is why? There is no easy answer to that question, but if we don't value God's blessing above all else, we sell our souls for a cheap substitute. [11]

> *The blessing of God...it's a decision to make, a habit to form,*
> *and a mindset to establish.* [12]
> ~ Mark Batterson

day three

Genesis 20

One of the things I love about Scripture is how God gives us the good, the bad, and the ugly. As Christ followers, it is so easy to fall into the trap of thinking we somehow fall short of the standard set by well-known Bible characters like Abraham, a trailblazer of faith who accomplishes so many great things for God. Yet, along his journey, we see him struggling to conquer repeated patterns of sin. His struggle with sin mirrors our own in so many ways, doesn't it? I am encouraged from accounts like Genesis 20 that God will use us even when we mess up and fall short of His glory. And He will go to great lengths to preserve and protect His people and His plan.

The last time we saw Abraham, he was standing in the place where he had interceded on behalf of Sodom and Gomorrah, watching the smoke rise from the smoldering cities. And now he is on the move again. For some reason, after he has lived in Hebron for years, Abraham packs up and moves south, to the land of the Philistines, enemy territory.

Warren Wiersbe writes:

> Gerar is just within Philistine country, but it was still a dangerous place to be. Perhaps it was the destruction of Sodom and Gomorrah that caused Abraham to want to move, but whatever his motive was, the decision was not a wise one. True, Abraham did not go down to Egypt as he had done before (Genesis 12). He was still within the boundaries of the land God promised to give him, but his move put him in a dangerous position. [13]

Read Genesis 20:1-2.

1. When Abraham arrives in Gerar, what does he say about his wife, Sarah, and what is the consequence? (v. 2)

As a result of Abraham's lie, King Abimelech unknowingly takes Sarah in to make her his wife. Abraham's cowardly conduct risks "Sarah's virtue and the purity of the promised seed." [14] But again, we see God's character as He intervenes dramatically, displaying His divine mercy as a Rescuer.

Read Genesis 20:3-7.

2. What does God do to prevent Abimelech from taking Sarah as his wife? (v. 3)

3. What is Abimelech's response? (vv. 4-5)

4. What is God's response? (vv. 6-7)

The next morning, Abimelech calls for Abraham and questions him about his lie regarding Sarah. His disdain with Abraham's choice is clear in verses nine and ten as he basically asks, "Whatever possessed you to do such a thing?"

Tragically, this is not the first time Abraham has lied about Sarah. As we saw in Genesis 12, Abraham did the same thing while they were in Egypt.

Bob Deffinbaugh makes this observation:

> The situation here is far more critical than in chapter 12. First, God has clearly revealed to Abraham and Sarah that together they will bear a son through whom the covenant promises will be realized. More than this, the conception of the child must be near at hand, for he was said to have been born within the space of a year (17:21; 18:10). Human reasoning would have considered the dangers in chapter 20 to be minimal since Sarah was long past the childbearing age (17:17; 18:11,13). But the eye of faith would have seen the matter in an entirely different light. Was Abraham's faith at a low ebb? It must be so. [15]

In a low faith move, Abraham decides it will be more effective to deceive Abimelech than to trust God. Relying on his own reasoning, Abraham makes assumptions and tells a half-truth.

5. What assumption does Abraham make? (v. 11)

Wiersbe gives us insight into Abraham's faulty reasoning:

> After arriving in Gerar, Abraham began to walk by sight and not by faith, for he began to be afraid. Fear of man and faith in God cannot dwell together in the same heart...Abraham forgot that his God was "the Almighty God" (Genesis 17:1), Who could do anything (Genesis 18:14) and Who had covenanted to bless Abraham and Sarah. [16]

Moreover, Abraham begins to explain his half-truth by saying that Sarah really is his sister, since they have the same father but different mothers. Let's pause here for a moment on the notion of half-truth. This takes me back to my early days of parenting. We all know the look on the face of a guilty child and how they begin grasping to plead their case. A sliver of a sentence holds a wee bit of truth or a minor detail may be left out to their advantage. What about as a friend or a wife? Perhaps we leave out a detail as we share something about someone else or even about ourselves, making it sound better or worse than it actually is? And one of the most common I hear from wives is the art of hiding recently purchased items. I have been in circles of women dozens of times who unashamedly brag about purchases they'd rather their husbands not know about. They devise elaborate schemes of hiding a new shirt in the back of the closet and then assuring him how old that thing is, or stashing things under the bed or in the attic, taking them out a little at a time.

God hates lies (Proverbs 6:17, 12:22). And, as Charles Spurgeon says, "God does not allow His children to sin successfully." [17]

Half-truths. Schemes. Giving part of the story or leaving part of it out. These sinful tactics are divisive and result in a guilty conscience, a tattered relationship, and a lack of trust on both sides. It can also bring about a tarnished character, a damaged testimony, and a lost ministry.

Make no mistake. God desires and requires that we recognize our sin, repent, and turn from it. The sad part of this account is that Abraham and Sarah did not deal with this same sin once and for all back in Egypt.

While this account may disappoint us as the reader, it also reassures us that our mistakes do not cast us out of God's plan and purpose. This is not a justification to sin by any means (Romans 6:1-2), but I have to believe God gives us these details in Scripture to encourage us to fully trust Him, to confess and repent of sin quickly, and to continue following Him with open hands, so He can use us for our good and His glory.

Read Genesis 20:14-18.

6. What does Abimelech graciously do for Abraham? (vv. 14-16)

7. What is the punishment for Abimelech's household as a result of Abraham's sin, and what does this tell us about our sin? (v. 18)

8. What happens as a result of Abraham's prayer to God? (v. 17)

Wiersbe says, "The fact that God answered Abraham's prayer for Abimelech is evidence that Abraham had confessed his sins and the Lord had forgiven him (Psalm 66:18-20)." [18]

Psalm 51:17 tells us, "The sacrifice you desire is a broken spirit. You will not reject a broken and repentant heart, O God" (NLT). Paul gives a similar message in 2 Corinthians 7:10, "Godly sorrow brings repentance that leads to salvation and leaves no regret…" (NIV).

As you close today, take a few moments to inspect your heart. Do you find yourself falling into the same sin patterns, maybe something generational? Do you overlook some sins as "small" like telling a half-truth? Could you be missing out on God's plan by holding on to sin and not forsaking it as Abraham and Sarah did?

If so, take a few moments to confess your sin to the Lord, no matter how big or small you may perceive it to be. Be assured, "until you and I are willing to deal with the sin in our lives, there is no blessing for us." [19] Ask Him to forgive you and strengthen you to completely forsake it. Confess to a trusted friend and ask her to pray for you.

Obedience is the first habit of highly blessed people. [20]
~ Mark Batterson

day four

Genesis 21

Is there a more beautiful truth to begin today's study than the opening words of Genesis 21:1? "The Lord kept His Word and did for Sarah exactly what He had promised" (NLT). What a reminder of our faithful God. He keeps His Word, and He does what He promises. Before you go any further in this lesson, stop and pray Genesis 21:1 back to the Lord as a declaration of praise for Who He is!

1. Reflect back to a time where you saw God keep His Word and promise to you.

Read Genesis 21:1-7.

A pregnancy twenty-five years in the making. Talk about waiting on the Lord! Can you just imagine Sarah's excitement as she finally holds this fulfilled promise in her arms? Verse 2 tells us that Isaac is born at God's "appointed" time. God's timing is perfect, and He can be trusted.

Ann Voskamp shares this insight about trust:

> We want things to go the way we choose—and God wants us to choose to trust His ways. We expect more—and God expects us to trust Him more. The ways God chooses for His chosen are ways that beg us to choose trust. It's impossible for us to please God unless we trust God with the impossible (Hebrews 11:6). There is no pleasing God without trusting God. Trusting God is no small thing: To God, it is everything. God wants to be chosen too. [21]

Not only have they waited a long time for Isaac to be born, but they are 100 and 90 years old! This is a miraculous birth. Paul tells us in Romans 4:19, "And Abraham's faith did not weaken, even though, at about 100 years of age, he figured his body was as good as dead – and so was Sarah's womb" (NLT).

Read Genesis 21:8-13.

Abraham prepares a feast to celebrate Isaac. His life is certainly cause for celebration, but here we also see tension rising.

2. What does Sarah witness and how does she respond? (vv. 9-10)

3. How does Sarah's demand make Abraham feel? (vv. 11-12)

In His graciousness, God comforts Abraham by reminding Him of the promise of Isaac and how He will also provide for his son, Ishmael. I love the tenderness of the Father in this text. I can imagine the tug in Abraham's heart as he dearly loves both of his sons and wants God's blessing for their lives. God steps in, as He faithfully always does, and seemingly says, "Abraham, I've got this."

Abraham awakens the next morning and makes preparations for Hagar and Ishmael as he sends them on their way with food and water. As the story unfolds, we continue to see the providential hand of God.

Read Genesis 21:15-21.

4. As they wander in the wilderness, what happens and how does Hagar react? (vv. 15-16)

And then verse 17 proclaims, "But God…" (NLT).

5. Look back to page 59 and record the meaning of Ishmael's name.

We read that God heard the boy crying, and this moved His heart to action. As I type these words, tears literally fill my eyes. This mother and son are alone in the wilderness, having just run out of water, afraid for their lives, I would imagine. Yet, they do not journey alone unseen and unheard. An angel from Heaven calls to Hagar.

6. What does the angel of God say to Hagar and what is she promised? (vv. 17-18)

7. How does God meet their needs? (vv. 19-21)

Let's pause here for a moment. I know that hundreds, likely thousands, of women will walk through the pages of Scripture covered in this study and relate to the cries of Hagar's heart. Are you wandering? Do you feel deserted? Alone? Afraid? Do you feel like you do not have the resources you need to survive…physically or emotionally? That deep, dark black hole that feels cold and endless. It seems no one sees. It seems no one hears. Surely, no one can understand this depth of pain and heartache. The hopelessness is so tangible and heavy.

Think of Hagar. She gets pregnant, not because she is wanted by her husband, but because she is part of a scheming plot to rush ahead of God's plan. Then, Sarah despises her. She feels like a burden, an outcast. Her son isn't the one everybody is excited about and looking forward to. And now, she has been thrown out. She is handed a bag of food and some water, and sent out to wander the desert alone, accompanied by this young, innocent, helpless boy. A boy who needs her, a boy who depends on her for sustenance and protection, a boy whom she dearly loves. How will she ever make it alone?

Overwhelmed, she bursts into tears. But God hears her. God sees her and He moves toward her. He comes right to where she is. And He will do the same for you. He is *El Roi*, the God Who sees. He is *Jehovah Shamma*, God is here.

Press into the heart of God. Hear His beating heart…for you.

The devil would have you doubt the very character of God and believe that you are alone, that God does not care, that you have done too much to deserve the attention of a holy God, or that your situation is too hopeless to be rescued and restored. The devil is a liar.

Press into the heart of God. Hear His beating heart…for you. Fall into His open arms. Take His holy hand and allow Him to set your feet on solid ground. Be convinced that He hears you, sees you, is with you, and is for you.

Waymaker, Miracle Worker.
Promise Keeper, Light in the darkness.
My God, that is who You are. [22]

8. How has God been a Waymaker for you <u>or</u> how will you trust Him, starting today, to be a Waymaker in your life?

Read Genesis 21:22-34.

God is continuing to bless Abraham and Sarah, as is evidenced by Abimelech's observation, "God is obviously with you, helping you in everything you do" (Genesis 21:22, NLT).

This is the blessed life that comes to the one who chooses the way of the Lord. In the remaining text of Genesis 21, we see Abraham making a covenant with Abimelech and choosing to be a peacemaker with his neighbor.

9. What does Abraham do to commemorate what God has done for him and what new name for God is introduced here?

Wells would disappear, trees would be cut down, ewe lambs would grow up
and die, altars would crumble, and treaties would perish,
but the Everlasting God would remain. [23]
~ Warren Wiersbe

The Blessing of a Hope-filled Future

For I know the plans I have for you, declares the LORD, plans to prosper you
and not to harm you, plans to give you hope and a future.
Jeremiah 29:11, NIV

Jeremiah 29:11 has become one of the most well-known and often quoted scriptures. It fills frames and adorns walls in many homes. But these words gave me life – literally – in the fall of 1995. Page 1,339 in my first ever study Bible is marked with a dried rose petal. This bright red, hard bound, now well-worn Bible was given to me by a dear pastor, primarily for the purposes of the religion classes I would take in college. I opened it late one night as a last resort, a measure of survival. It was a lifeline to my soul. And in reality, it saved my life.

God brought me to this verse as a college sophomore during a time that was laced with pain, doubt, loss, hopelessness, loneliness, and deep heartache. I remember the small room with white painted cinder block walls, a comforter with bright sunflowers adorning my bed, and a heavy heart that I could barely stand any longer. While I was not following the Lord closely at this time in my life, my Firm Foundation took me to the pages of God's Word. I knew I needed Him…He was all I had in that split moment. Reading these words from Jeremiah, really from the heart of God, pulled my head above water and gave my weary heart a glimpse of hope.

Life did not magically get better. In fact, I had many years ahead with more trial and pain, but this verse had been etched onto my heart and mind, and in the most uncertain of times, the Holy Spirit brought it back to me, tossing a life preserver of truth at those times I needed it most. This verse would reassure me, in the darkest of days, that He *knew* the plans He had for me, and that *His* plans were good and would only give me hope and a future. I clung to this hundreds of times over the course of many years. Still to this day, it is my most treasured verse and fills my heart with warmth and assurance like no other. And it always takes me back to the night in that tiny dorm room when God first introduced me to this promise.

Reflect back on this week's study. In the life of Lot, his family, and Abraham and Sarah, we see faithlessness, discouragement, fear, and doubt. While they did not have these words of Jeremiah before them, God had spoken and made Himself known in other ways. He had given them clear instructions and expected them to trust and obey.

We can relate to their choices in times when we've taken matters into our own hands or chosen a path that was not in line with God's will. Perhaps you find yourself right now in circumstances that beckon you to set human reasoning above God's reasoning. Or maybe, like me, you're able to reflect back on a time in your life when a reminder of God's goodness and faithfulness pulled you up out of a pit.

1. How does the promise of Jeremiah 29:11 speak to your heart today and how can you apply it to present circumstances?

Approximately ten years later, I would find myself blessed to be part of a discipleship group that altered my way of studying the Bible, looking for the character of God on every page. So much of what I read was familiar, but He was beginning to speak to me in new ways. I'd read and heard Ephesians 3:20 before, but as I came to see His Father heart even more clearly, this verse was like a fire hydrant, giving me more than I could take in. "Now to Him who is able to do immeasurably more than all we ask or imagine, according to His power that is at work within us..." (NIV). The NLT says it this way: "Now all glory to God, who is able, through His mighty power at work within us, to accomplish infinitely more than we might ask or think."

As a part of discipleship, I was also learning how to pray – boldly, confidently, with authority, and by praying Scripture. This, coupled with my new insight into God's Word, set me on a path to pray Ephesians 3:20 in everything! My assurance from years back that God had good plans for me, coupled with His power to do more than I can even imagine, set my heart ablaze. I have not walked this path faultlessly. Oh, how I have flailed around at times, falling into the trap of doubt and fear and anxiety. But the difference now is that the Holy Spirit quickly prompts my heart to come back. My time of staying hunkered down in the cave of despair is less and less frequent.

So, let me ask you some questions. Better yet, allow the Holy Spirit to ask you. Journal your heart on these pages as an offering of yourself to Almighty God. Lay your soul bare before Him.

- Do you trust God's plan for your life?

- Do you believe He has *good* plans for you?

- Do you believe He is able to _____?

- Do you trust that He can do more than you ask or imagine?

- Does your life reflect a heart that trusts Him and His ways?

Blessed to Be a Blessing

So far in our study we have focused on how we can be a blessing to others, but this week I would like us to take a little bit of a different approach. Take a moment today to sit before the Lord and ponder who He is, in light of Jeremiah 29:11 and Ephesians 3:20. Thank Him specifically for how He has spoken to you this week through Bible study and revealed Himself to you. Thank Him for His perfect plans for your life, His promise of His goodness, His abundance, and His provision. And then ask Him to reveal someone in your life who has been as life-giving to you as these verses were for me. Her name probably came to mind the moment you read the sentence. Someone who has been a blessing to you.

This week, reach out to that person. It can be a written letter, a text message, or a phone call. Let her know when and how she blessed you and what that meant for you. Be a blessing in her life by letting her know just how much she has blessed you.

You and I can rest in assurance of His perfect love and His perfect plan.

We have been abundantly blessed! We have been given the right to become children of God! We have a Savior, Who came to give us abundant life, not just the kind of life that keeps us hanging on by a thread. You and I can rest in assurance of His perfect love and His perfect plan, even when we cannot see how He's working in the midst of it all.

Even when there is no visual evidence of God at work, I promise you,
God is watching over His word to perform it. [24]
~ Mark Batterson

five

ABRAHAM IS TESTED
Genesis 22-23

I have learned to kiss the wave that throws me against the Rock of Ages. [1]
~ Charles Spurgeon

We have been blessed to raise two boys who are now grown with families of their own. I loved being a momma and continue to have a heart for those of you who are still in the trenches, because let's face it, training up children in the way they should go is not for the faint of heart! One moment you are confident in your maternal instincts and aware you are in a holy partnership with the Lord raising Kingdom kids, and the next you are convinced you should have tried your hand at raising puppies instead!

When I think back to my days raising little boys, memories flood my soul causing a knot to rise up in my throat. Tears tend to flow freely as I recall those years with great fondness. Time is kind and tends to erase some of the more difficult days, causing my memories to be cast in a rosy glow that is generally less than accurate, but more delightful to indulge in.

As I take a trek back down memory lane, I am reminded of the time when our oldest son was a mere two years old. For Christmas, his grandparents purchased tickets for us to take him to see *Sesame Street Live* at the Mid-South Coliseum, a facility with about 10,000 seats. At that time, there were few options for children's programming, so he regularly watched Sesame Street, and was greatly enamored with the talking puppets. Even at his young age, he was completely engrossed with the familiar characters, as they regaled their young audience with stories and dance numbers.

At intermission, my husband took him for a bathroom break and visit to the snack bar. Unbeknownst to me, our little guy dropped his daddy's hand and slipped away in the crush of parents and little people crowding in to buy refreshments. My husband raced towards him, but lost him in the crowd. As I was sitting in our seats, I caught sight of a security guard on the far side of the building holding the hand of a little one. The guard's eyes were scanning the audience, but because of the angle I could not see the child. I immediately began to pray.

It was apparent to me that a toddler had been separated from his parents. My mother's heart went out to the panicked mom and frantic dad that were surely racing wildly around the auditorium, looking for their darling. The narrator announced that the lights would soon dim for the second act and urged all of his little friends to get ready to come back to Sesame Street. Just then, my husband tapped me on the shoulder to deliver the news, "Jason slipped away from me in the crowd. I have alerted security. Come help me look." His words took my breath away, but in an instant, I realized that the family I had been praying for was my own! I grabbed my husband's arm and waved frantically to the security guard shouting, "Here. We are here." A joyous reunion ensued, although our little sanguine two-year-old wasn't the least bit frightened. In fact, he was thrilled to have been paraded around the coliseum, meeting all sorts of new people and making friends.

As I read the account of Abraham offering Isaac that we will be studying in this lesson, my mind drifted back to that night. I can still feel the fear that seized my heart when I heard our son was missing. My throat tightens and my heart pounds at the memory. As I try to step into Abraham's story and bring you with me, I am reminded that I cannot fully grasp the enormity of the emotions or the implications of such an act of obedience. There are great lessons of faith to be learned as we walk through this passage. As we dig in, prepare to be amazed!

day one

Genesis 22:1-3

To get the flow of the story, read Genesis 22:1-19, but today we will only be considering the first three verses.

God orchestrates circumstances in our life to reproduce Christ in us through the testing of our faith. This truth chafes us and pulls at our sensibilities of who God is and how He operates in His Kingdom. Would a loving God allow devastating trials to come into the lives of believers? Beloved, the cold hard fact is that God is after our <u>holiness</u> and not merely our <u>happiness</u>. Because His work in our lives often runs counter to our flesh-driven desires, we frequently find ourselves at odds with His design as we long to be content and comfortable.

Years ago, I was exposed to this vital truth: happiness is the byproduct of holiness. Happiness is something you stumble over when you are chasing hard after Jesus, when you are pursuing personal holiness and practical righteousness, when you are leaning into Jesus, and when you are walking by faith and desiring holiness through obedience. I can testify to the truth of this statement in my own life and on the basis of God's Word. Proverbs 29:18 says, "Happy is he who keeps the law." In the Sermon on the Mount, Jesus said, "Blessed are those who hunger and thirst for righteousness, for they shall be satisfied" (Matthew 5:6). [2]

At first glance, the story of Abraham offering Isaac is shocking. Not only is God's requirement to offer Isaac as a burnt offering staggering, but Abraham's obedience is also stunning. It is hard for us to wrap our brains around this account in Abraham's life, but I can assure you we will uncover an abundance of glorious truth that will leave us breathless in the presence of God!

Happiness is the byproduct of holiness.

Of this passage, Chuck Swindoll writes:

> Genesis 22 reveals a man with a treasure so valuable, so cherished that it threatened to compromise his relationship with God. He didn't treasure money or possessions. He didn't treasure his calling. He didn't even treasure a dream. His long-awaited son, Isaac, was his treasure, and he would have sacrificed anything for that young man. Never doubt it; Abraham adores his son! [3]

Read Genesis 22:1.

1. Who is the Author of Abraham's test? (v. 1)

We have seen Abraham, a man with a nature like ours, rise to the heights of super-saint, and we marvel at his unwavering faith. Considering his background and upbringing, we rejoice to read of his resolute acts of obedience after becoming a God-follower. However, the Old Testament pages are replete with his failures. As we read these accounts of failure, we typically find ourselves scoffing at his immaturity, clucking our tongue and pointing our finger at such poor judgment and outlandish behavior. Is it possible we are so quick to judge him because we recognize this pattern in our own lives? How grateful I am that God records Abraham's successes along with his failures, cautioning us to avoid his pitfalls.

Concerning tests of faith, Swindoll explains:

> God is, of course, omniscient. He knows the future as accurately as He knows the past. He doesn't put people to a test to see how well their faith responds under fire; He prepares tests of faith to show us what He has made of us lately. Where we pass or fail, we learn about ourselves. We learn where we need improvement, or we discover how spiritually mature we have become. [4]

Beloved, there is a distinct difference between trials (or tests) and temptations. Warren Wiersbe says, "Satan tempts us to bring out the worst in us, but God tests us to help bring out the best." [5] Trials can quickly turn into temptations if we respond incorrectly.

Let's look back at James 1:2-3 for more insight into this important aspect of the Christian life.

2. What is our response to be when trials prevail? (v. 2)

3. When we properly respond to a trial, what is the end result? (v. 3)

The prevailing thought conveyed in this passage is that God sends various trials in order to grow our faith.

Now, read James 1:13-15.

In these verses, James shifts gears to write about temptations. The devil tempts us in an area of fleshly desire in an effort to cause us to sin. God tests our faith. Satan tempts us to sin.

4. When we give way to the temptation of the enemy, what is the result? (vv. 14-15)

Peter picked up on the same theme in his first letter. Read 1 Peter 1:6-9.

5. Why does Peter say we greatly rejoice in the midst of various trials? (vv. 8-9)

Now, let's return to our story in Genesis 22 as we consider the test God has designed for Abraham. Please note that God calls Abraham by name, a reminder that God's tests are custom made for each child of God and every experience is unique.

And don't overlook the fact that when God calls him, Abraham responds, "Here I am." Abraham's response indicates that he has an intimate relationship with God and is well acquainted with His voice. We also sense Abraham's commitment to obedience.

When we were raising our boys, we repeatedly impressed upon them that we were looking for immediate obedience. We taught them that when we called them, we expected to hear, "coming," followed by the sound of little feet moving towards us. There would be no counting to three or yelling or threats. They would be expected to respond quickly and fully. Failure to do so would result in appropriate consequences. To all the young moms out there, this took about 18 years, give or take, so don't lose heart. It's a long process!

6. What does God ask of Abraham? (v. 2)

Notice that God does not reveal Abraham's final destination. This is reminiscent of Genesis 12:1 when God said, "Go forth from your country…to the land which I will show you." In Genesis 22:2, God told him to "go to the land of Moriah…[to] one of the mountains of which I will tell you." Is it possible that this is to remind Abraham of God's past faithfulness? We can't know for sure, but it is a plausible explanation. In the midst of a test, if we are able to reflect on God's history of faithfulness, it strengthens our resolve and allows us to move ahead in faith.

It is nearly impossible for us to fully grasp the magnitude of God's request. As a parent, my mind races with the anguished questions, and I can easily imagine the thoughts that ran unfiltered through Abraham's mind. Certainly, we would not have thought less of Abraham if he had argued with God or collapsed in a heap while sobbing. Or if he had begged God to take his life instead of that of his son. But that is not what Abraham does. As John Phillips observes, "We see no indication of hesitation, no reluctance, no distance, no argument, no bargaining, no pleading, no delay whatever." [6]

I have heard it said, "Faith must be tested in order to be trusted." James said, "Faith without works is useless…was not Abraham our father justified by works when he offered up Isaac his son on the altar? You see that faith was working with his works, and as a result of the works, faith was perfected" (James 2:20-22). We are saved through faith, not works. Ephesians 2:8-10 says, "For by grace you have been saved through faith; and that not of yourselves, it is the gift of God; **not as a result of works**, so that no one may boast. For we are His workmanship, **created in Christ Jesus for good works**, which God prepared beforehand so that we would walk in them" (emphasis mine). Good works do not save us, but they will naturally follow a genuine conversion experience. Abraham's walk of faith is demonstrated by his obedience to God's revelation and his works of righteousness.

In the same way, we are called to demonstrate the genuineness of our salvation by a life of personal holiness and practical righteousness.

Genesis 22:4-14

From his own personal experience, David was able to write, "Weeping may last for the night, but a shout of joy comes in the morning" (Psalm 30:5). Difficult situations seem to be magnified by the dark. From the account in Genesis 22:1-3, it appears that God speaks to Abraham concerning the sacrifice of Isaac during the night. I think we can safely assume the father does not get any sleep, but rather spends a restless night in prayer, asking for God to give him the strength to walk in obedience to His command.

Read Genesis 22:4-14 and let's unpack this passage together.

While we might assume Abraham will delay as long as possible, the Scripture says he "rose early in the morning" (Genesis 22:3) to prepare for the journey, emphatically trusting the "God who cannot lie" (Titus 1:2).

On the third day as they approach Mount Moriah, Abraham tells the two young men who are accompanying them to remain at the base of the mountain with the donkey.

1. Don't overlook this incredible testimony of faith found in Abraham's instructions to the young men. Reread Genesis 22:5 and make note of Abraham's declaration of faith.

2. Hebrews 11:17-19 gives us some insight into what Abraham believes about his son and his God. According to this passage, what does Abraham believe concerning Isaac? Concerning God?

We are left to marvel at the faith of Abraham, but let's not overlook the faith of Isaac. By this time, he is a young man, perhaps in his late teens or early twenties. At any rate, he is old enough and strong enough to carry the wood necessary for an altar up the mountain and he could have easily resisted his aged father. Genesis 22:6 says, "Abraham took the wood of the burnt offering and laid it on Isaac his son, and he took in his hand the fire and the knife." The sudden weight of the wood brings home to Isaac the part he will play in the drama looming ahead. He watches with pained eyes as he sees his father take the fire and the knife. Isaac is familiar with altars and sacrifices. He has been raised by God-worshiping parents and has participated in the preparation of slaying countless sacrificial lambs for burnt offerings to the Lord God. There is no doubt that Isaac is aware of what lies ahead. Phillips insightfully notes, "We can see him look at his father – at that wise, old face now so drawn and strained – and in that face read something the like of which he has never seen before." [7]

Presumably the young man walks beside his father in silence, both men deep in thought. The quiet is broken when Isaac poses the awkward, probing question Abraham has been dreading all along, "Behold, the fire and the wood, but where is the lamb for the burnt offering?" (Genesis 22:7).

As readers of this Old Testament account, we begin to hold our breath as we watch father and son trudge up the steep incline. Isaac is thoroughly submitted to his father's will, even as Abraham is surrendered to His Father's. Amid the anguish of Abraham's soul, there is also a settled confidence in the Lord, who will provide.

Abraham builds the altar, arranges the wood, binds his son, and lays him on the wood. As he stretches out the knife to slit the throat of his son, "the angel of the Lord" (Genesis 22:11), who is a pre-incarnate appearance of Jesus, calls him by name. Again, Abraham answers, "Here I am." God stays his hand and says, "Now I know that you fear God, since you have not withheld your son, your only son, from Me" (Genesis 22:12). Only then does Abraham see God's provision, a ram caught in the thicket.

3. According to Genesis 22:13, what does Abraham do?

4. What does Abraham name the place at the top of the mountain? (v. 14)

Before father and son have set out on their trek up the mountain, the Lord has divinely intervened and prepared a substitute!

We are not told how Abraham or Isaac respond to the supernatural provision of God, but we can assume a great shout of joy gave way to loud exclamations of praise and worship, which may have dissolved into tears of gratitude.

We live in a rural area and springtime is always a glorious sight to behold. Recently, I took a walk to try to enjoy the cool spring temperatures before the sweltering heat of our southern summers descends on us. Along the way, I was stopped in my tracks by a peony bush near my driveway which was in full bloom. The white blossoms were so heavy that they caused the stems to bow down to the ground, but that did not diminish their loveliness. It only served to accentuate the lush greenery and magnify the crisp white petals of each blossom.

We live on property that my parents bought in the early 70's with the intention of building a home after my dad retired. My folks lived in East Memphis and were longing for the country life. In 1981, my dad had a one-car garage with an attached workshop built near the site of their future home. My father was a talented woodworker and his plan was to have a nice area to work on his creations. He added electricity, water, a septic system, and a very tiny bathroom. My mom planted the peony bush along with some of her other favorite perennials, intending them to grow into mature plants by the time they made the move. Sadly, soon after my dad's retirement, he fell ill and their plans changed. Their house was never built, and the little garage/workshop was used primarily for storage. After my dad's death in 2000, my mom rarely visited the property.

In 2010, an economic downturn caused our family business to fail. We gave up our business and our home. With no real options available, we moved into my folks' one-car garage. We did not have a kitchen, laundry hook-ups, or a closet, but with the sheer determination of pioneer homesteaders and the knowledge that our God is faithful, we moved in and began a renovation project that took five years to complete. We were fixer-uppers long before it was the trend!

My folks are both home with the Lord now. As I stood and looked at my mother's prized peony bush in all its glory, I marveled that long before she ever knew that we would live on the property, she had planted a shrub that I would be enjoying after she was gone.

When my folks bought the undeveloped land in Moscow, TN shortly after Craig and I married, they could have never dreamed that we would need a place to live in 2010. But God knew.

When my dad decided to have a one-car garage with an attached workshop built, he could have never imagined that one day it would be our home. But God knew.

When my dad made the decision to run electricity, dig a well and put in a septic system to the little garage, he could have never dreamed that one day we would need them. But God knew.

When my dad thought that adding a gravel drive would make easier access to the little garage, it couldn't have crossed his mind that one day, we would be grateful for his decision. But God knew.

When my dad decided to over-insulate the little garage and put in nine-foot ceilings, he could have never in his wildest dreams known that one day these decisions would prove to be beneficial for us. But God knew.

When my mom thought she might begin to plant some of her favorite flowers on the property so that they might mature into large specimens for her future home, she could not have possibly known that I would be the beneficiary of her green thumb. But God knew.

So, I stopped. And I pondered. And I considered how the Lord had gone before us and prepared a place long before Craig and I would need it. I blessed Him. I praised Him. I worshiped Him. Because God knew and He is a God who provides!

This Old Testament passage came to mind, "Then it shall come about when the Lord your God brings you into the land which He swore to your fathers, Abraham, Isaac, and Jacob, to give you, great and splendid cities which you did not build, and houses full of all good things which you did not fill, and hewn cisterns which you did not dig, vineyards and olive trees which you did not plant, and you eat and are satisfied, then watch yourself, that you do not forget the Lord Who brought you from the land of Egypt, out of the house of slavery. You shall fear only the Lord your God; and you shall worship Him and swear by His name" (Deuteronomy 6:10-13).

God knows, and "The Lord Will Provide" (Genesis 22:14). He is our *Jehovah-Jireh*! Note that the translation of *Jehovah-Jireh* is not "The LORD Did Provide," but "The LORD Will Provide." In other words, the name is not merely a commemoration of a past event; it is the anticipation of a future act. *Jehovah-Jireh* pictures God's eternal <u>prevision</u> and His continual <u>provision</u> for His children.

Take a few minutes and reflect on your walk with the Lord. Think of a time when He has prepared the solution before you even realized the problem. Perhaps it is not as dramatic as a bankruptcy and a place to live, but recall a time when God staggered you with His provision.

5. Write down that memory and turn it into a time of praise and thanksgiving. God knows our needs and He provides.

Long before Abraham and Isaac were aware of their need for a substitute, God caused a ram to become entangled in a thicket, and held it there until the problem and the provision met in a divinely orchestrated moment in time. The Genesis 22 passage is one of the clearest pictures of the substitutionary death of the Lord Jesus Christ, the Lamb of God, recorded for us in the Old Testament. But I am getting ahead of myself. In tomorrow's lesson we are going to dive deep into this rich passage, and see the message in type and picture of the death, burial, and resurrection of Christ!

day three

Genesis 22

The story of redemption is woven throughout the entire Bible. From Genesis to Revelation, Scripture is clear – God's remedy for man's ruin is through the substitutionary death of Jesus Christ. All who are willing to come to Him in repentance and faith are gloriously redeemed, sealed with the Holy Spirit of promise, and guaranteed Heaven as their final destination. These truths are easily identified in the New Testament, as the Lord Jesus and His teachings are front and center.

However, in the Old Testament, Jesus is presented in picture, or type, which takes some careful investigation in order to accurately discern Him. A cursory reading may cause us to inadvertently overlook His presence in the pages of the Old Testament. But He is there, working in the lives of people, calling them to repentance and faith, and creating multiple opportunities for salvation by grace through faith, to which Hebrews 11:1-2 attests, "Now faith is the assurance of things hoped for, the conviction of things not seen. For **by it the men of old gained approval**" (emphasis mine).

Before we dive into today's reading, my caution is this – when we see a picture of Christ in the Old Testament, we must be careful not to take the picture too far or it will collapse. For instance, Moses is a picture of Christ, but he was born with a sin nature (inherited from Adam), and he disobeyed God on several occasions. Christ, however, "knew no sin to become sin on our behalf, so that we might become the righteousness of God in Him" (2 Corinthians 5:21).

Although we have already looked at the story of Abraham offering Isaac before the Lord, the portrayal of Christ in this passage, lying just below the surface, is too rich to ignore and demands a second look. As a student of the Word of God for over 40 years, I love to study. I long ago became aware that the more I learn, the more there is to learn. Never is that truth so real to me as it is when I study the Old Testament in depth. Discovering pictures, types, and prophecies of the Lord Jesus in the Old Testament is particularly rewarding.

Today, I invite you to join me on a walk through the entire chapter of Genesis 22, this time looking for pictures of our precious Savior, Jesus Christ.

Read Genesis 22.

In this passage, Abraham is easily seen as an Old Testament picture of God the Father, as Phillips makes clear:

> Where, within all the covers of God's blessed Book, is there a chapter like Genesis 22 for displaying what Calvary meant to God the Father? We turn to Psalm 69, Isaiah 53, and Psalm 22 to see what Calvary meant to the Son. But it is Genesis 22 that shows us what Calvary meant to the Father. "Take now thy son, thine only son Isaac, whom thou lovest, and get thee into the land of Moriah; and offer him…upon one of the mountains." Over and above the demand for Isaac was the ultimate demand for Jesus. All that Moriah meant to Abraham in terms of agony and heartache and pain; that a thousand-fold, ten-thousand-fold, is what Calvary meant to God. [8]

While Abraham is a picture of the Father, Isaac is a type of Jesus, the Son. Adrian Rogers explains, "Isaac, in the Old Testament, pictures, prophesies, and foretells the coming of the Lord Jesus Christ, God's promised miraculous Son." [9] Let's consider the parallels between Isaac and Jesus.

Both Isaac and Jesus fulfill a promise, have a miraculous birth, and are named before they were born.

- Isaac is the long-promised son to Abraham (see Genesis 12:3; 18:9-10).

- His birth is a miracle. "Now Abraham and Sarah were old, advanced in age; Sarah was past childbearing" (Genesis 18:11). Isaac is miraculously conceived.

- Isaac is named before he was born. In Genesis 17:19, God speaks to Abraham, saying, "Sarah your wife will bear you a son, and you shall call his name Isaac; and I will establish My covenant with him for an everlasting covenant for his descendants after him."

1. Read Genesis 3:15, Isaiah 7:14, and Matthew 1:21. Make note of the similarities between Isaac and Jesus Christ.

Both Isaac and Jesus are only sons.

2. What description is given to Isaac in Genesis 22:2?

As we know, Isaac is not the only son born to Abraham. But, while he may have fathered Ishmael, God makes it clear that Isaac is the son of the promise He made to Abraham (Genesis 17:19-21), the son whom He acknowledges, and, at this point, he is the only son in Abraham's tribe (Genesis 21:9-14).

3. How is Jesus described in John 3:16?

Pause for a moment and ponder what depths of love the Father has for you that would cause Him to sacrifice His darling Son to redeem you.

We cannot fully fathom Abraham's heart of obedience that would embrace the sacrifice of his only son, the son of the promise. Likewise, we can never truly process the love of God for us, as guilty sinners, that would cause Him to give us His only Son as a substitute to atone for our sins. What we can do is enter into His sacrifice by repentance and faith.

Both Isaac and Jesus bear the burden.

Genesis 22:6 tells us that once Isaac and Abraham reach Mount Moriah, Isaac carries his own wood. Wiersbe explains that the "wood seems to be a picture of sin that Jesus bore for us (1 Peter 2:24)." Abraham took the wood and "laid it on Isaac his son" (Genesis 22:6). God, the Father, "laid on Him [Jesus] the iniquity of us all" (Isaiah 53:6). [10]

Both Isaac and Jesus ask their father a question.

4. Do you remember from our study yesterday what Isaac asks Abraham? (v. 7)

5. How does Abraham answer the question? (v. 8)

When Abraham responds, he does not know how and when God will provide, but with unwavering faith he believes the promise of God. Although Isaac is old enough and strong enough to overtake his father, Isaac willingly continues on his journey, submitting to his father.

6. Read Matthew 27:46. What question does Jesus ask His Father?

We do not know what is occuring within the Godhead at this intense moment. However, in a way that is beyond our understanding, Jesus is experiencing a distance, a sense of "forsakenness," in His connection to the Father as He takes on the sins of mankind.

Both Isaac and Jesus have to die.

In Genesis 22:9, Abraham prepares the altar, arranges the wood, and lays his son on the altar. With halting breath, Abraham raises the knife into the air. But then, the Lord directs Abraham to "a ram caught in the thicket by his horns" (Genesis 22:13). Here the picture changes.

Isaac has prophetically represented Christ up to this point. Now he pictures all of us who are in need of a Savior. The ram becomes a picture of Jesus, the Substitute for the sin of lost humanity. God had indeed provided "the lamb for the burnt offering" (Genesis 22:7). Jesus Christ, the Lamb of God, would become the once-for-all-time Sacrifice for sin! Wiersbe writes, "In Isaac's case, a substitute died for him, *but nobody could take the place of Jesus on the cross.* He was the only sacrifice that could finally and completely take away the sins of the world." [11]

7. Genesis 22:15 tells us that the angel of the Lord calls out to Abraham a second time. He reminds Abraham of His covenant promises. What are they? (vv. 17-18)

Reflecting on this beautiful Old Testament portrayal of the sacrifice of Christ for us, Phillips writes:

> Thus, the Holy Spirit paints for us one of the very greatest pictures of Calvary in the Bible. The unforgettable experience of Abraham and Isaac at Moriah had its sequel. The voice of God rang out again, confirming all the blessings that God had already bestowed on Abraham and his seed. With that fresh confirmation ringing in their ears, the father and the son found their way back to where the young men waited. From there they journeyed back to the place of the well, to Beersheba in the south. [12]

The chapter ends with a reference to the children born to Abraham's brother, Nahor (Genesis 22:20-24). This genealogy is intended to introduce Rebekah into the story. We will have to wait until next week to dive into the story of a bride for Isaac. Until then, rejoice believers! We have been redeemed! Hallelujah! What a Savior!

day four

Genesis 23:1-20

We cannot be certain how many years have passed since Abraham's test of faith on Mount Moriah and the next test he will face in Genesis 23, but scholars agree that the two accounts are separated by a number of years. Genesis 22 focused on Abraham's offering of his only son, Isaac. Now, Genesis 23 opens with Sarah's obituary.

Read Genesis 23:1-2.

1. How old is Sarah when she dies? (v. 1)

Together, Abraham and Sarah have shared a rich life together following their God. The two weathered the storms of life as well as the consequences of some rather poor decisions on both of their parts. After decades of being married, it is not surprising that Abraham weeps when she dies. Dr. Rogers paints the picture for us, "I want you to see this scene. I want you to see this noble, old man. I can imagine him with long white hair, and a flowing beard, and a marvelous countenance, as the tears course down the deep ravines in his cheeks and soak that white beard as he looks into the lifeless face and the cold clay of the body of Sarah." [13] Truly, Abraham's heart is crushed with sorrow as the memories of their life together flood his mind.

F.B. Meyer gives us perspective into Abraham's grief:

> [Sarah] was the only link to the home of his childhood. She alone could sympathize with him when he talked of Terah and Nahor, or of Haran and Ur of the Chaldees. She alone was left of all who...had shared the hardships of his pilgrimage. As he knelt by her side, what a tide of memories must have rushed over him of their common plans and hopes and fears and joys! He remembered her as the bright young wife, as the fellow pilgrim, as the childless persecutor of Hagar, as the prisoner of Pharoah and Abimelech, as the loving mother of Isaac, and every memory would bring a fresh rush of tears. [14]

In the shadow of his beloved wife's death, Abraham, in his humanity, is in pain. But although death has torn her from his arms, it cannot and could never tear her from his heart. Wiersbe notes, "Grieving is one of God's gifts to help heal broken hearts when people we love are taken from us in death." [15] However, we do not grieve as those "who have no hope" (1 Thessalonians 4:13), because for believers "to be absent from the body" is "to be at home with the Lord" (2 Corinthians 5:8).

Wiersbe tells a story about talking with the late Vance Havner shortly after his wife, Sarah, died. Both men were speaking at a conference at Moody Bible Institute, and Wiersbe approached Havner and said, "I'm sorry to hear you lost your wife." Havner looked at him, smiled, and replied, "Son, when you know where something is, *you haven't lost it.*" [16] Selah.

This is the first mention of tears in Scripture, and tears will not end until God will one day wipe away every tear, "and there will no longer be *any* death; there will no longer be any mourning, or crying, or pain" (Revelation 21:4). What a day that will be!

As all of us who have walked through the death of a loved one know, there is "a time to mourn" (Ecclesiastes 3:4), and then there is a time to resume living. What happens next gives us insight into life in the ancient world.

Read Genesis 23:3-9.

2. What does Abraham request from the sons of Heth (the Hittites)? (v. 4)

After all the years Abraham has lived in Canaan, he still doesn't own any property in the Promised Land. He calls himself a "stranger and a sojourner" because that is how he feels. He doesn't even own a burial plot, so he must haggle with the sons of Heth before he can bury his wife.

3. What do the Hittites call Abraham? (v. 6)

While the Hittites do not worship the God of Abraham, they have a deep respect for the man, and they offer for him to have one of their best caves for Sarah's burial plot, since he is a "mighty prince."

4. What is Abraham's response to their offer? (v. 9)

Read Genesis 23:10-20.

Lots of back and forth bargaining goes on in these verses. Abraham is clear in his intentions – he wants to purchase the cave of Machpelah from Ephron who is present in the crowd at the city gate, the typical place where business was conducted. When Ephron offers to "give" the land to Abraham, it is not a sincere gesture. He is just throwing it out there to see how Abraham will respond. As he listens, Abraham learns that Ephron does not want to sell the cave apart from the field where it is located. So, he offers to buy both the cave and the field before he even knows the price. Genesis 23:16-18 reads almost like a deed of purchase with the agreed upon price (400 shekels of silver), the details of the property (the cave, the field, the trees), and the witnesses (the Hittites who watch the transaction take place). Only after purchase is complete, does Abraham bury Sarah "in the cave in the field of Machpelah near Mamre (which is at Hebron) in the land of Canaan" (v. 19).

Abraham's desire to bury Sarah in Canaan is not just a sentiment. It is a statement of his faith. He does not want to take Sarah back to their homeland of Ur to be buried. He believes that one day his descendants will possess the land he has been sojourning for decades. God has promised him that, and he is fully convinced that God will keep His Word.

Read Hebrews 11:8-10.

5. According to this passage, what was Abraham looking and longing for?

Like Abraham, we are pilgrims, just passing through. This world is not our home. We, too, are looking for "the city which has foundations, whose Architect and Builder is God" (Hebrews 11:10).

6. When you die, how do want your loved ones to remember you?

Oh friend, may we live in such a way that at the end of our lives there will be no regrets from love unexpressed or no shame from sin unaddressed. As we view our death, or the death of a loved one, as a "graduation to glory," earthly sorrow will be swallowed up in heavenly praise. Death does not exhaust the promises of God. Speaking of Abraham, Sarah, and their descendants, the writer of Hebrews tells us:

> All these died in faith, without receiving the promises, but having seen them and having welcomed them from a distance and having confessed that they were strangers and exiles on the earth. For those who say such things make it clear that they are seeking a country of their own. And indeed, if they had been thinking of that country from which they went out, they would have had opportunity to return. But as it is, they desire a better country, that is, a heavenly one. Therefore, God is not ashamed to be called their God; for He has prepared a city for them (Hebrews 11:13-16).

Like Abraham and Sarah, when we die, the promises of God will live on. Every promise He has made will one day be fulfilled. That is why Paul was able to say, "O death, where is your victory? O death, where is your sting?" (1 Corinthians 15:55).

Until then, may we live by faith, so that we can die by faith, because "when you die by faith, you have a wonderful future." [17] Truly, truly, the best is yet to come!

day five

The Blessing of Obedience

Blessed is a man who perseveres under trial; for once he has been approved,
he will receive the crown of life which the Lord has promised to those who love Him.
James 1:12

Even as I sit at my computer and crank out these words, I am in the midst of a health crisis. A diagnosis of breast cancer in the fall of 2021 caused our world to spin out of control – at least temporarily. As my husband and I sought the Lord, He helped us regain our spiritual equilibrium and obtain an eternal perspective in what we immediately identified as a testing of our faith. While I cannot adequately reconcile the timing of this test or articulate the "why" of it, I am thoroughly convinced that my God is in control. "For this reason, I also suffer these things, but I am not ashamed; for I know whom I have believed, and I am convinced that He is able to guard what I have entrusted to Him until that day" (2 Timothy 1:12). I would be remiss if I did not tell you there have been dark days, anxious thoughts, and sleepless nights, as we have tried to process what God called us to in this season of suffering. As we have determined to walk in obedience to Him, we have been able to build trust in His sovereignty and abide in His lovingkindness.

One of the pitfalls of being in the midst of a God-ordained test is comparing your test to someone else's difficult season.

1. Why are we prone to do this and what are the ramifications of such mental gymnastics?

Every test of faith is very specifically designed by the Father in order to produce a desired outcome. Genesis 22:1 says, "God tested Abraham." James 1:2 refers to the various trials we will encounter as "the testing of your faith." God is orchestrating the events of our lives, including the testing of our faith, in order to create within us the likeness of His Son.

As we have walked through this season of suffering, the Lord has raised up so many of His people to minister to us and to pray for us. We have been overwhelmed by the outpouring of kindness. We have especially been stunned by the number of women who have had a shared experience. They have spoken comfort and encouragement into my life, refreshing my soul and strengthening my resolve. 2 Corinthians 1:3-4 says, "Blessed be the God and Father of our Lord Jesus Christ, the Father of mercies and God of all comfort, who comforts us in all our affliction so that we will be able to comfort those who are in any affliction with the comfort with which we ourselves are comforted by God."

2. What season of suffering has the Lord walked you through as He tested your faith?

3. How has He allowed you to comfort others who have or are experiencing similar tests?

4. As you choose to walk in obedience, how does God bless you?

Blessed to Be a Blessing

While it typically takes some space and time to realize your test can be a blessing in order to bless others who are coming along behind you, gaining this insight can give you an eternal perspective on your suffering. Stepping into someone's pain is always difficult, whether it is to share your testimony of a common experience, to meet a practical need, to become a prayer warrior on their behalf, or to sit in silence displaying the ministry of presence.

This week I want to encourage you to seek out a woman who is going through a "testing of faith." Prayerfully ask the Lord what would minister to her in the most beneficial way. Her testing may or may not be with her health – it could be in her marriage, with a child, in her job, or in some other area. Create a blessing plan for your "person" with 3-5 specific ways you can minister to her. Then, get started this week blessing her.

May the Lord bless you for blessing her in Jesus' name!

ISAAC IS MARRIED
Genesis 24-25:18

There is no more lovely, friendly or charming relationship,
communion or company, than a good marriage. [1]
~ Martin Luther

Generally speaking, a wedding is an extremely happy event for the bride and groom. Although my husband and I were married in 1974, I can still recall the sweetness of the day. We were married at Bellevue Baptist Church, which was at that time located in midtown Memphis.

Dr. Adrian Rogers had recently come to pastor our church and served as the officiant of our wedding. Family and friends gathered in the Lee Auditorium to join us in our joyous ceremony. All was right with the world, until we slipped into the reception hall ahead of our guests. Unbeknownst to us, the bakery which my parents had contracted with to provide our tiered wedding cake and groom's cake had written down the wrong date, and no cakes had been prepared to serve our guests. Since this was back in the day when nuts and mints were the only accompaniment to the cakes, this was disastrous! My mother contacted the bakery just before the wedding ceremony began to inquire about the cakes. They were understandably horrified when their mistake was realized. To rectify the situation, they promised to bring cakes from a wedding scheduled for the following day. True to their word, the bakery arrived with the wedding cakes just before our guests descended the stairs to attend the reception.

My new husband and I had been ushered downstairs to the fellowship hall ahead of our guests. Bakery workers were frantically assembling the cake layers and piping pale blue roses in a vain effect to create some semblance of what we had ordered. Adding to this fiasco, the groom's cake was a white sheet cake with a plastic bride and groom on the top. To distinguish the fact that this was indeed a groom's cake, they had added a ball and chain to the ankle of the groom as a symbol of marriage that I still, to this day, do not find funny! I was able to shrug this disaster off because at the end of the day, I was married to the great love of my life and, frankly, that was all that mattered to me. But my poor mother! For her, it was a personal failure. For the rest of her life (she lived to be in her 80's), she could still vividly recall this disgraceful event with all the visceral anger she felt on that day, and she continued to hold a very serious grudge against the bakery!

Despite this fiasco, the marriage has survived – for better, for worse, for richer, for poorer, in sickness and in health, to love and to cherish both now and forever!

In this lesson, we are looking at the love story of Isaac and Rebekah. To understand this story, we will need to go back across some forty centuries to a place called Mesopotamia. In ancient biblical times, arranged marriages were the norm (and remain so in many Eastern cultures today). In some instances, the young man and woman may have been allowed to participate in the matchmaking process, and to a degree, some may have been able to decline a marriage proposal, as is the case in Isaac and Rebekah's story. But for the most part, it was the parents who selected the mate for their child.

As we dig into the story of Abraham securing a bride for Isaac, we will also note the picture of God the Father, preparing a bride for His Son, the Lord Jesus Christ. Keep that storyline in mind and get ready to be amazed!

Genesis 24:1-9

This story begins with an anxious Abraham, who is concerned about carrying on the family name. Let's walk with him as he goes about securing a bride for Isaac.

Read Genesis 24:1-4.

Abraham has lost his great love, Sarah. If she had married Abraham at the age most young girls were given in matrimony at that time, she would have been a young teen, possibly around 15. If so, at her death at 127, the couple would have been together for over 112 years! As Abraham is coming to the end of his own life, he knows well the blessing a godly wife has been to him. He believes the promise God has made to bring forth a great nation through his son, and from that great nation, to bless the world. But for that promise to be fulfilled, Abraham must not only have a son, but the son must be married, and from the marriage have children. To help us understand the urgency of the matter, Abraham is now 140 years old (Genesis 21:5; 25:20), and Isaac is 40. It is past time for Isaac to have taken a bride! Although we cannot be sure why Abraham has allowed his son to reach the age of 40 without obtaining a bride for him, it is possible that God has used the death of Sarah to remind Abraham of the fleeting nature of time.

1. What does Abraham request of his servant? (vv. 2-4)

2. What two specific instructions does Abraham give his servant regarding Isaac's wife-to-be? (vv. 3-4)

Abraham is aware of the importance of his choice for Isaac. Isaac's bride must be a woman who is "capable of appreciating the importance of God's covenant – someone who would help Isaac be a good steward of this great honor. He wants Isaac to marry a woman with the same kind of strength and dignity he has enjoyed in Sarah for more than a century." [2] Certainly, many Canaanite women would have jumped at the chance to marry Isaac, knowing the wealth and prestige that would accompany such a union. But the aged patriarch knew a suitable helpmeet would not be found among the Canaanite women. John Phillips explains Abraham's concern: "The daughters of Canaan were a worldly, wicked, wanton crowd with no knowledge at all of the true and living God. They were snared in the most frightful forms of pagan idolatry. There could be no thought of Isaac marrying one of them." [3] The woman who will marry Isaac must come from within the family of God.

Although the Pentateuch (the first five books of the Bible) has not been written yet, Abraham understands God's prohibition against intermarriage with pagans.

3. Read Deuteronomy 7:3-4. God prohibits His people from marrying unbelievers. What is the consequence of such an unholy alliance?

This principle is also reiterated in the New Testament.

4. Read 2 Corinthians 6:14-18. Why should believers not be unequally yoked with unbelievers?

Note: The admonition for believers not to be unequally yoked in marriage (as well as other relationships) is certainly valid, and the consequences of ignoring such a warning can be severe. However, I am also aware that perhaps this is the position some of you find yourself now. Should this be your present marital circumstance, I can assuredly tell you on the authority of God's Word that God's very best for you is to remain in your marriage (see 1 Corinthians 7:12-16 and 1 Peter 3:1-7). If you find yourself in a difficult marriage, or in the midst of extenuating circumstances such as abuse or adultery, I encourage you to seek the help of a godly counselor.

Read Genesis 24:5-9.

Although the text does not reveal the servant's name, most scholars presume he is Eliezer, so for the sake of this lesson, we will refer to him as such. We are introduced to Eliezer in Genesis 15:2 when Abraham calls him "the heir of my house." Abraham, who is childless at this point, highly regards Eliezer and intends to leave his fortune to him. God makes it clear that Abraham will have a biological son and "he shall be your heir" (Genesis 15:4). Even after the birth of Isaac, Eliezer remains a faithful servant to Abraham, which provides proof that his service is not based on what he might gain from his master, but what he could do for him. Throughout the years, Eliezer has been Abraham's head of operations, his financial consultant, an overseer of his amassed wealth, and most likely his closest friend. Charles Swindoll notes that Eliezer has "been involved in the life of Abraham for decades, so he knew the aging patriarch as well as anyone." [4]

Understandably, Eliezer has some hesitation about his assignment.

5. What concern does he express to Abraham? (v. 5)

Abraham is confident in the Lord. For 65 years He has guided and blessed Abraham, and He will not fail him now. Abraham is resting in God's ability to direct his servant to the woman of God's choosing: "The LORD, the God of Heaven, Who took me from my father's house and from the land of my birth, and Who spoke to me and Who swore to me, saying, 'To your descendants I will give this land,' He will send His angel before you, and you will take a wife for my son from there" (Genesis 24:7).

Like Abraham, we can trust in the Lord to direct our paths. The Bible is replete with texts that support this truth, but I have chosen a couple of my favorites for us to look at in closing today.

6. Read Proverbs 3:5-6. What can we learn about walking with the Lord from this passage?

7. Look up Psalm 16:11. What can we learn about the Lord's dealings with us?

Beloved, we can trust the Lord. As we walk in obedience to His Word and dependence upon His Spirit, we can confidently know, like Abraham, that He will guide our steps. Hallelujah! What a Savior!

Today, we will travel with Eliezer on his expedition to find a bride for Isaac.

Read Genesis 24:10-21 as we join him on his journey.

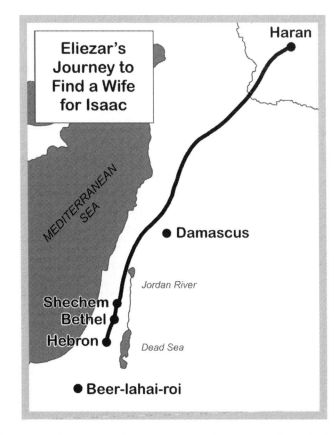

Abraham's servant "set out with a variety of good things of his master's in his hand; and he arose and went to Mesopotamia, to the city of Nahor" (Genesis 24:10). Warren Wiersbe draws our attention to the servant's commitment to serve Abraham and fulfill his requests: "His favorite name for Abraham was my 'master,' which he used nineteen times in this narrative. He lived and served only to please his master, and that is a good example for us to follow today." [5] Abraham's homeland is approximately 500 miles north. This will be a lengthy and arduous journey, but the servant will gladly obey his master.

By this time, Eliezer is advanced in age himself, having served Abraham for many years. Moses does not reveal any facts about his journey, but we can surmise that Eliezer and his traveling companions arrive road-weary, with a pack of tired and thirsty camels. I can only imagine how exhausted he was from being bounced along on the back of a smelly camel, with its uneven gait and nasty habit of spitting!

1. How many camels are on the journey with Abraham's servant? (v. 10)

2. What is significant about the time Eliezer stops outside of the city at the well? (v. 11)

3. What is the first thing Eliezer does when he stops at the well? (v. 12)

The servant knows that he needs divine guidance to find a wife for Isaac. He does not ask God for a miraculous sign, rather he seeks direction from God through an ordinary event in the ancient world.

4. As he prays, what does Abraham's servant request that Isaac's future bride say when he asks her for a drink of water? (v. 14)

Before Eliezer finishes praying, he sees Rebekah, the granddaughter of Abraham's brother, Nahor, coming to fill her water pots. In order to arrive at the well before Eliezer finishes praying, she more than likely had left her house before the servant even began to pray. Kent Hughes explains that "we are meant to see that the providence was all of God. That is, as the servant humbly prayed, God directed him to ask for specific providences that God was at the same time orchestrating as Rebekah arrived at the well amidst his prayers." [6] This is a biblical example of God's promise in Isaiah 65:24, "It will also come to pass that before they call, I will answer; and while they are still speaking, I will hear."

As he watches Rebekah approach, Eliezer is evaluating the young woman. Bob Deffinbaugh explains why Eliezer believes Rebekah may be the bride he is seeking for Isaac:

> She was the daughter of Bethuel, Abraham's nephew. Beyond this, she was a beautiful woman who had maintained her sexual purity – essential to the preservation of a godly seed. Seemingly, she was the first to appear and the only woman there at the moment. Everything the servant saw suggested that this woman was a candidate for the test he had devised. [7]

Running to Rebekah, Eliezer asks for a drink of water, which she gladly serves him, perhaps recognizing he has traveled a great distance. What happens next is one of my favorite parts of this story. "Now when she had finished giving him a drink, she said, 'I will draw **also** for your camels until they have finished drinking'" (Genesis 24:19, emphasis mine). Rebekah reveals a bit of her good and godly character by volunteering "to draw also" for the camels – to go over and above what was asked of her. Hughes gives us colorful insight into what it was like for Rebekah to water the ten camels:

> To grasp what a wonder this was, we must understand that the ancient well was a large, deep hole in the earth with steps leading down to the spring water – so that each drawing of water required substantial effort. And more, a camel typically would drink about twenty-five gallons of water, and an ancient water jar held about three gallons of water. This means that Rebekah made between eighty to one hundred descents into the well. As to the amount of time she gave to this, a camel takes about ten minutes to drink its full complement of water. Rebekah's labors filled one and one half to two sweaty hours! [8]

And all the while, the servant watches without saying a word, to see whether or not she really is the woman God has for Isaac.

Read Genesis 24:22-49.

Only after all the camels have been watered does Eliezer speak. Deffinbaugh explains,

> While the woman's evident beauty may have satisfied the standards of lesser men, the test was to be allowed to run its course. Adorning the woman with golden gifts, the servant proceeded to determine her ancestry. When this qualification was satisfied, the servant bowed in worship, giving the glory to God for His guidance and blessing. [9]

5. What questions does Abraham's servant ask Rebekah? (v. 23)

Rebekah takes her gifts and runs home to tell her parents and her brother about the generous stranger who needs a place to sleep for the night.

6. Who is Rebekah's brother? (v. 29)

Insight into Laban's character is revealed in verse 30, when the "gold ring weighing a half-shekel and two bracelets [on] her wrists weighing ten shekels in gold" (Genesis 24:22) catch his eye. No doubt, he takes note of the treasures Eliezer and his men have brought from Abraham as he unloads them from the camels. I think we can safely assume Laban is eager to see a deal struck and a dowry exchanged for his sister's hand in marriage! In the years to come, Isaac and his son, Jacob, will discover more about the rogue character of Laban.

Verse 33 tells us that Eliezer refuses to eat until he has explained the purpose of his journey. On the heels of such a difficult trip, this serves to reiterate the urgency he feels concerning his mission to find a bride for Isaac.

Now, the task at hand for Eliezer is to convince this family that Abraham's son is the right man for Rebekah. Accepting the marriage proposal will result in a move that would put hundreds of miles between her and her parents. Will her family allow her to go? Will Rebekah agree?

As Eliezer begins to speak, he identifies himself as "Abraham's servant" (v. 34), setting "aside many objections of these relatives, who were concerned to protect the purity of Rebekah's descendants." [10] Then, he relays how the Lord has blessed Abraham with "flocks and herds, and silver and gold, and servants and maids, and camels and donkeys" (Genesis 24:35). This will ensure Isaac's ability to provide abundantly for the needs of Rebekah, and affirm Abraham's faith in his decision to leave his homeland and follow after God to a land He would reveal. Finally, Eliezer recounts his commissioning from Abraham and his first encounter with Rebekah. The response now rests with her father, Bethuel.

As today's lesson draws to a close, I am reminded how the Lord guides our steps as we prayerfully and obediently seek after Him. Before Eliezer had arrived in Nahor and dismounted his camel, the maiden Rebekah had loaded up a water jar on her shoulder and begun to make her way to the well outside the city gates of Nahor. It was typically the time when women went to draw water, but on this particular day she appears to have arrived alone. As Rebekah stepped into Eliezer's line of vision, he was whispering a prayer in his heart to The God Who Provides concerning a bride for Isaac. In a sovereignly orchestrated moment, God's provision and Eliezer's prayer came together in a divine encounter.

Are you seeking God's direction in an area of your life right now? As you faithfully pray and look to Him, He will guide you. Walk in the truth the Father reveals to you today and He will take care of the rest.

day three

Genesis 24:50-67

Having walked with God for over 40 years, my husband and I can look back on our faith journey and see many times that the Lord directed our paths, although oftentimes we were unaware of Him orchestrating circumstances to bring about His perfect will. Many random decisions were made along the way, some so mediocre that I cannot even remember seeking the Lord concerning the matter. The staggering thing is that often, those seemingly disconnected choices would come together to create a divine appointment. Without realizing it, God was causing "all things to work together for good" (Romans 8:28) in a situation that would only be revealed in His perfect timing.

Equally mysterious is how God can take seemingly bad situations and redeem them, producing His good and perfect will from broken places. Let's reflect back on Abraham's story.

Only God can turn a mess into a miracle in order to further His Kingdom!

Soon after God's call, Abraham (then called Abram) took his family and "set out for the land of Canaan" (Genesis 12:5). When a famine hit, he took a disastrous detour into Egypt. There, ruled by fear, Abraham lied about his wife, calling her his sister. Sarah (then called Sarai) was taken into Pharaoh's house. Genesis 12:16 tells us that Pharaoh "treated Abram well for her sake; and gave him sheep and oxen and donkeys and male and female servants and female donkeys and camels" (Genesis 12:16). While we cannot be totally sure, this appears to be the time when Eliezer joined Abraham's household. He most likely fought alongside Abraham and aided in the rescue of Lot and his family after their abduction from Sodom. As we saw in Genesis 15:2, Eliezer has risen to a place of honor and prestige prior to the birth of Isaac as "the heir" of Abraham's house. And ultimately, it was Eliezer (we assume) that sought a bride for Isaac. God took a bad decision on Abraham's part and used it for His good. Beloved, only God can turn a mess into a miracle in order to further His Kingdom!

1. Can you recall a time when you made a misstep and God redeemed the situation for your good and His glory? Record your thoughts on how God moved on your behalf.

Now, let's get ready to walk through part two of the Isaac and Rebekah love story when they will finally meet.

Read Genesis 24:50-61.

Eliezer's rehearsal of the events that have brought him to ask for Rebekah to be given in marriage to Isaac is met with Laban's and Bethuel's consensus that this is indeed a God-ordained union. Abraham's servant then gives them a bounty of rich gifts. But then, when morning comes, Laban and his mother begin to have second thoughts.

2. How many days do Rebekah's mother and brother want her to wait before she leaves to meet Isaac? (v. 55)

True to his character, the servant remains steadfast in his desire to complete his master's mission. Hughes writes, "God honored the servant's resolve because the family's attempt to stonewall him occasioned another joyous providence – the public declaration of Rebekah's faith." [11]

3. When Rebekah is consulted about her wishes, what is her reply? (v. 58)

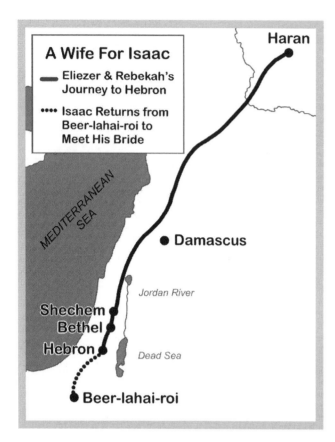

A Wife For Isaac

— Eliezer & Rebekah's Journey to Hebron

•••• Isaac Returns from Beer-lahai-roi to Meet His Bride

Haran

MEDITERRANEAN SEA

● Damascus

Jordan River

Shechem ●
Bethel ●
Hebron ●

Dead Sea

● Beer-lahai-roi

Her simple consent is a reflection of her trust in the God of Abraham. And with her "I will," it is time for the group to depart.

The blessing that Rebekah's family gives her parallels the blessing given to Abraham after he offers Isaac on Mount Moriah: "Indeed I will greatly bless you, and I will greatly multiply your seed as the stars of the heavens and as the sand which is on the seashore; and your seed shall possess the gate of their enemies" (Genesis 22:17). According to God's wonderful plan, the same blessing is given to Isaac and his future bride, Rebekah.

Read Genesis 24:62-67.

Imagine how difficult this long, hot journey is for the young bride-to-be. And her mode of transportation? A camel. Enough said.

Meanwhile, Isaac is anxiously awaiting word to discover if a bride had been procured for him. We find him out in the field in the early evening, meditating. In the distance, he can barely make out the silhouette of camels, carrying his betrothed. As he walks towards her, Rebekah dismounts and covers herself with her veil. Swindoll clarifies:

> According to custom, brides-to-be wore a veil. By pulling her veil across her face, Rebekah signaled that she was his bride. As a red-blooded male, Isaac wanted to know what kind of face he would be staring at for the next several decades. Because of their marriage rituals, however, it was common for a groom to have no idea what his bride looked like until their wedding night. [12]

Eliezer recounts to Isaac how the Lord revealed his bride, Rebekah, how the marriage deal was struck, and how she and her nurse have returned with him. Moses then summarizes the next events, "Isaac brought her into his mother Sarah's tent" and "took Rebekah" as his wife (v. 67). Isaac loves her, and as a sweet aside, she comforts him after his mother, Sarah's, death. Swindoll notes, "The tent once used by Sarah was more spacious and ornate than the others and would have remained empty after her passing. By taking Rebekah into his mother's tent, Isaac communicated to his new wife and to the rest of the community that 'she is now the mistress of the household.'" [13]

As women, we all adore a love story. We want to read "and they all lived happily ever after" and believe it is so. And if that is all the story of Isaac and his bride, Rebekah, represented in the legacy of Abraham and Sarah, we would be intellectually and emotionally satisfied. But, like the Old Testament account of Abraham sacrificing Isaac, this is a multi-layered story with rich theological New Testament truths that bears revisiting. Dr. Adrian Rogers said, "The Old Testament says somebody is coming. The New Testament says somebody has come. The book of Revelation says somebody is coming again. And the entire Bible is the story of the Lord Jesus Christ." [14]

In Genesis 22, Abraham was tested when God told him to sacrifice his son. On Mount Moriah, Abraham's son, Isaac, in a figure, died. He was raised again on the third day. Now he needs a bride. His father seeks a bride for Isaac. I remind you that Abraham is a picture of the Father and Isaac is a picture of the Son, the Lord Jesus. And the servant, whom we believe is Eliezer, is a lovely picture of the Holy Spirit. "The very word *Eliezer* itself means 'God's helper.'" [15] In John 14:16, Jesus said, "I will ask the Father, and He will give you another Helper." Rebekah is an Old Testament portrait of the Bride of Christ. She is described as a beautiful virgin (Genesis 24:16). The Bride of the Lord Jesus is to be a chaste bride, a pure bride, a virgin bride.

4. In the Bible, marriage is a picture of the union between Christ and His Bride, the church. Read Ephesians 5:22-33. What can we discover in this passage about the relationship between Christ and His Bride?

Only those whose sin has been washed away through repentance and faith in the Lord Jesus can become a part of the Bride of Christ through His imputed righteousness.

By faith, Rebekah left her father and mother and all that was familiar in order to go with Eliezer. Her brother and mother wanted her to wait ten days before leaving, but this appears to be a distraction in order to delay obedience. However, Rebekah was determined to go. This speaks to the requirement to make an individual I decision to enter into a personal relationship with Jesus. Remember that Rebekah had never seen Isaac. She has only heard about him through his servant, Eliezer. Peter, who had been an eyewitness of the Lord Jesus, wrote, "Though you have not seen Him, you love Him, and though you do not see Him now, but believe in Him, you greatly rejoice with joy inexpressible and full of glory" (1 Peter 1:8).

Nothing is written of Eliezer's interaction with Rebekah along the way, but we can imagine he told her all about Isaac. And oh, how she would have wanted to hear about her intended!

In his message entitled, *A Bride for Isaac*, Dr. Rogers added this nugget as he imagined what the journey to Canaan looked like:

> And then you know what he'd do? All the way, along this trip, he had a treasure chest. It was just filled with jewels: diamonds and rubies and bracelets. Every now and then, when the journey would get a little long and a little dreary, with a twinkle in his eye, he'd reach in this treasure chest, he'd pull out a beautiful gem, he'd hand it to her and say, "This is from Isaac" – And this is what he'd do: he'd just take the things that belonged to Isaac and show them unto her. And the Bible mentions this: that he kept on giving to her these presents.
>
> And, you know, that's what the Holy Spirit does. That's what He does! Ah, when I got saved, when the Lord said to me, "Will you go with this man? Will you follow the Holy Spirit, even though you've never seen the Lord Jesus Christ? Will you go?" I said, "Yes, I'll go." And every now and then, the road, you know, it gets a little weary sometimes. It gets a little dusty, and it gets a little dreary. But then the Holy Spirit of God opens up the treasure chest of the Lord Jesus. And every now and then, He'll reveal some gem to my heart. I'll be studying the Bible, and I'll come up with a golden nugget. I'll be reading the Bible, and I'll come up with two fistfuls of diamonds. And, oh, I'll be in prayer, and the Lord will just bathe me in His love, and I'll say, "Thank you, Spirit of God, for revealing to me about my Master, the Lord Jesus Christ." Oh, how sweet the journey is! We haven't seen Him, but the Spirit of God just makes Him real to us. [16]

Beloved, I pray today's study has caused you to worship as you consider how much the Father loves you and desires a personal relationship with you. I trust your heart has been warmed as you have reflected on what Jesus Christ has done for you. I pray you have been stirred as you contemplated the Holy Spirit's role in your salvation and your sanctification. And above all, I trust you have not overlooked the beautiful picture of the Second Coming of Christ tucked away in the pages of the Old Testament. Isaac "lifted up his eyes and looked, and behold" (v. 63), his bride was coming. And she "lifted up her eyes" (v. 64) and behold, her bridegroom was coming for her. One of these days, dear one, the Father will send His Son to receive His Bride. Then the cry will ring out, "Behold the bridegroom! Come out to meet Him" (Matthew 25:6). Together, we will celebrate at The Marriage Supper of the Lamb and be in His presence forever and ever!

> *The Spirit and the bride say, "Come." And let the one who hears say, "Come." And let the one who is thirsty come: let the one who wishes take the water of life without cost."*
> Revelation 22:17

And together we say, "Even so, come, Lord Jesus" (Revelation 22:20, KJV).

Hallelujah! What a Savior!

day four

Genesis 25:1-18

With Genesis 25, we come to the last chapter in Abraham's life. Called to serve the Lord at the age of 75, Abraham had cut ties with his family, pulled up his Mesopotamian roots, and started out on his pilgrimage. And now, one hundred years later, he is still going strong.

Read Genesis 25:1-11.

1. What does verse 1 tell us about Abraham?

His new wife's name is Keturah, and it means "incense" or "she who makes incense to burn….Keturah, we would like to believe, was the kind of woman whose life evokes worship in others. She would lift heavenward, like ascending incense, the thoughts of those around. We cannot wonder that Abraham, in his loneliness, was attracted to a woman like that." [17] Perhaps this speaks to the fragrance of God resting on her life, or the sweetness of her personality, but at any rate, Abraham is drawn to her and takes her for his wife.

We cannot be certain how many years have elapsed between Isaac's marriage and the opening of this chapter. We can assume that as the patriarch watches his son and Rebekah settle into their new lives together, Abraham longed for the love and companionship of a mate. Swindoll writes, "While romantics would have Abraham feel the pangs of Sarah's loss for another thirty-eight years, God granted him the grace to experience a fresh romance with another godly woman. (I know she was godly because Abraham would not have chosen anyone less.)" [18]

Abraham may have thought his life was over after the death of Sarah, but God has some new experiences in store and a few surprises as well! After experiencing years of infertility with Sarah, Abraham's second marriage produces six more sons, seven grandsons, and three great-grandsons according to this lineage recorded in verses 2-4.

With the years of his life waning, Abraham wisely decides to ensure the succession of the covenant.

2. Although Abraham has remarried and had other children, to whom does he leave his fortune? (v. 5)

Abraham's marriage to Keturah does not change the fact that Isaac is "the promised son – the one whom God said would be the sole heir of the covenant, the one through whom the Hebrew nations would be born." [19]

Genesis 25:6 says, "To the sons of his concubines, Abraham gave gifts while he was still living, and sent them away from his son Isaac eastward, to the land of the east." It appears that to protect Isaac's inheritance, the children of Keturah were considered to be the sons of a concubine.

Swindoll sheds some light on this confusing verse:

> According to the tradition of many ancient cultures, concubines were often female servants in a household who became part of the family and bore children for the patriarch. They typically enjoyed all the rights and privileges of a wife, but a legal wife outranked them. Furthermore, the children of a legal wife did not have to share their inheritance with the offspring of concubines.

> Abraham most likely took Keturah as a wife in the fullest sense of the word, and the Bible offers no evidence that he ever shared a marital bed with more than one woman after his error with Hagar. Keturah was his wife in every way that mattered, but he considered her a concubine to protect Isaac's inheritance. "Abraham gave everything he owned to his son Isaac" (Genesis 25:5).

> Obviously, this refers to his estate after he died. Before he died, he took good care of all his children, establishing each of his sons financially as they left the nest and started families of their own. He had evidently learned from the mistake he made with Ishmael and Hagar, who he had sent away with inadequate provisions. Having repented of that earlier sin "he gave gifts to the sons of his concubines and sent them off to a land in the east, away from Isaac" (Genesis 25:6). [20]

By sending the sons of Hagar and Keturah away, Abraham is making sure that no one will be able to contest Isaac's claims in the future.

3. How old is Abraham when he dies? (v. 7)

4. The Bible records his obituary in verse 8. What is said of Abraham?

In an interesting aside, the Bible states that "his sons Isaac and Ishmael buried him" (Genesis 25:9). Some temporary truce must have been reached between the step-siblings to facilitate the burial of their father. Abraham had always held a special place in his heart for Ishmael, his son born out of impatience when the promise of God seemed to be waning (Genesis 16).

Read Genesis 25:12-18.

These verses record the lineage of Ishmael, containing the names of his 12 sons. From these tribes sprang the Arab people who are, to this day, Israel's worst enemies. An interesting commentary on Ishmael and his descendants is included in verse 18. Deffinbaugh comments:

> The land of Canaan was not to be the possession of Ishmael nor of his descendants; rather we are told: "And they settled from Havilah to Shur which is east of Egypt as one goes toward Assyria; he settled in defiance of all his relatives" (Genesis 25:18). In this verse one more promise is shown to be fulfilled, the promise God made to Hagar years before: "And he will be a wild donkey of a man, His hand will be against everyone, And everyone's hand will be against him; And he will live to the east of all his brothers" (Genesis 16:12). [21]

Oh that Ishmael had turned to the God of Abraham and followed in his father's footsteps! Phillips remarks, "Of all the countless thousands of families on the earth in those days wrapped in pagan darkness and superstition, it was Ishmael's remarkable privilege to have been born into a home where the truth of God was known and obeyed. He was born of a man who became known in Scripture as 'the friend of God.'" [22] Ishmael is without excuse for his rejection of God.

Beloved, while this is not the time for a discussion of adult children and their decisions, I am well aware that many of you have prodigal children or grandchildren. May you continue to saturate Heaven with your prayers for your prodigal (see Luke 15:11-32) to return to the faith you hold dear.

Abraham died and left behind a precious testimony of a life well lived. For over 100 years, he had been a stranger and a pilgrim on the earth. He was a sojourner, a tent dweller, living in God's Promised Land, but never fully possessing it. We know that through the door of death, Abraham stepped out of this world into the realm of glory and eternity with Christ Jesus.

Death, even for believers, is shrouded in mystery. With our limited ability, we do not fully comprehend what the Bible teaches about eternity, but we can joyfully concur with Paul's assessment, "For to me, to live is Christ and to die is gain" (Philippians 1:21). The psalmist said, "Precious in the sight of the Lord is the death of His godly ones" (Psalm 116:15).

5. Sadly, many believers needlessly fear death. Read Hebrews 2:14-15. In His incarnation, Christ was victorious over death. What can you learn about death from this passage?

6. Paul addresses the mystery of life after death for the Christian in 1 Corinthians 15:50-58. What does this passage teach us?

Unlike Solomon, who started strong but ended poorly, Abraham finished strong for the Lord. Although he stumbled along the way in his faith walk, he stalwartly repented and returned to the Lord God. "Abraham's death shows what faith can do for a man. He died in peace (see Genesis 15:15); he died 'full' (satisfied), and he died in faith (Hebrews 11:13)." [23]

As we wrap up our study on this passage, my heart is still rejoicing as I ponder eternity with Christ! One day, all those who have put their faith in Christ will join with the "myriads of myriads, and thousands of thousands, saying with a loud voice, 'Worthy is the Lamb that was slain to receive power and riches and wisdom and might and honor and glory and blessing'" (Revelation 5:11-12).

I close with this benediction and blessing:

> Now to Him who is able to keep you from stumbling, and to make you stand in the presence of His glory blameless with great joy, to the only God our Savior, through Jesus Christ our Lord, be glory, majesty, dominion and authority, before all time and now and forever. Amen (Jude 1:24-25).

day five

The Blessing of Perseverance

*We count those blessed who endured. You have heard of the endurance
of Job and have seen the outcome of the Lord's dealings, that the
Lord is full of compassion and is merciful.*
James 5:11

While most all of us, as children of God, desire to leave the shallows of the early Christian experience behind and wade out into the deep things of the Lord, we are not fully conscious of the high cost required. We crave comfort. We shrink back from challenges, difficult people, and above all, suffering. But we cannot learn perseverance unless our faith is tested. A hard truth to embrace, but one that has been played out in the life of every saint who has developed spiritual maturity. Franklin D. Roosevelt is reported to have said, "A smooth sea never made a skilled sailor." [24]

**We cannot learn
perseverance unless
our faith is tested.**

Throughout Abraham's life, he persevered in faith. Through triumph as well as failure, the friend of God kept moving forward in his faith for 100 years. And suffice it to say, he was a different man at 75 than he was at 175.

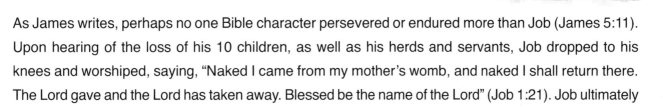

As James writes, perhaps no one Bible character persevered or endured more than Job (James 5:11). Upon hearing of the loss of his 10 children, as well as his herds and servants, Job dropped to his knees and worshiped, saying, "Naked I came from my mother's womb, and naked I shall return there. The Lord gave and the Lord has taken away. Blessed be the name of the Lord" (Job 1:21). Job ultimately lost his wealth, his health, his friends, and quite possibly the most painful of all, his wife's support. Job had no way of knowing the spiritual warfare that was taking place in heavenly places, yet he continued to trust in God. "Though He slay me, I will hope in Him," declares Job (Job 13:15). Like Abraham, Job's ironclad faith in the One True God enabled him to endure, faithful to the finish.

Blessed to Be a Blessing

Reflecting on the personal trials I have experienced walking with the Lord for over 44 years, I can testify that the woman who entered the trials is not the same one who exited them. Through seasons of difficulty, we learn to persevere. We learn to rely on the grace of God. We build a history of trusting God's faithfulness, even when we cannot discern His purpose and sometimes cannot sense His presence. Paul writes, "Therefore I am well content with weaknesses, with insults, with distresses, with persecutions, with difficulties, for Christ's sake; for when I am weak, then I am strong" (2 Corinthians 12:10).

1. Ask the Lord to give you the name of a person you know who is in a hard place, but is persevering. Write down Scripture verses that you will commit to pray for him or her.

2. What are some practical ways you can minister to this precious one and be a blessing? As James 5:11 tells us, "The Lord is full of compassion and is merciful." Will you be the hands and feet of God and minister to this dear one with compassion and mercy?

3. Now, turn your thoughts into deeds and do something to bless your person. Right now. Today.

None of us are getting out of this sin-cursed world without experiencing hardship. It is a hard reality, but true nonetheless. Next time you find yourself in a difficult season, go to the Throne of Grace and receive from the Lord what you need to persevere. Hebrews 4:16 says, "Therefore let us draw near with confidence to the throne of grace, so that we may receive mercy and find grace to help in time of need." Rest in the fact that God has a divine purpose and that He will work out His plan in His time, for our good and for His glory!

seven

ISAAC IS BLESSED
Genesis 25:19-28:9

God is sovereign. His grace cannot be tamed. [1]
~ Kent Hughes

With the death of Abraham, the chain of patriarchal history continues through his son, Isaac. Isaac's prominence as a patriarch appears to be overshadowed by his famous father, Abraham, and his strong-willed son, Jacob. Even though Isaac lives longer than his father or his son, Moses devotes twelve chapters to the life of Abraham, ten chapters to Jacob, and only six chapters to Isaac (and even those are attached in some way to Abraham and Jacob). But, lack of prominence does not equate with the absence of significance.

Isaac's life is "part of the divine plan that eventually produced the Jewish nation, gave us the Bible, and brought Jesus Christ into the world." [2] If that does not describe a significant life, I don't know what possibly could!

Warren Wiersbe makes this apt observation, "There are more Isaacs in the world than there are Abrahams or Jacobs, and these people make important contributions to society and to the church, even if they don't see their names in lights or even in the church bulletin." [3] A person's legacy is not built upon the accolades they receive, or thankfully, the mistakes they make. What makes a person unforgettable is the difference he or she makes in the lives of others. Although Isaac is a quiet man who never goes into battle, and never travels far from his birthplace, he goes down in history as a hero of the faith, a patriarch of Israel, and a covenant keeper. Let's spend some time getting to know him better!

Genesis 25:19-34

After Abraham dies, Isaac becomes the sole heir to Abraham's material wealth. But more importantly, Isaac receives spiritual wealth from his parents, "knowing and trusting the true and living God and being a part of the covenant blessings that God had graciously bestowed upon Abraham and Sarah and their descendants." [4] Just imagine what it was like as a boy to watch and learn from his father, the man God called His friend (Isaiah 41:8). And what it was like for him to be rescued from death by God on Mount Moriah. I seriously doubt that he ever looked at a ram or a thicket again without being reminded of that day!

Read Genesis 25:19-26.

Genesis is divided by ten uses of the Hebrew word *toledot*, translated "generations." [5] Five of the records frame primeval history, the other five provide the structure for patriarchal history. With the *toledot* in verses 19-20, Moses introduces the lineage of Isaac, Israel's second patriarch.

1. What age is Isaac when he marries Rebekah? (v. 20)

2. How many years are Isaac and Rebekah married before they have children? (vv. 20, 26)

After hearing from Isaac that God was going to make a great nation out of their offspring, and that his seed would be like the stars in the sky and the sands on the seashore, Rebekah would have anticipated to be pregnant soon after they married. And do you remember her family's blessing as she left home to marry Issac? "May you, our sister, become thousands of ten thousands, and may your descendants possess the gate of those who hate them" (Genesis 24:60). Month after month, year after year, those words echo in her heart and mind. A promise and a blessing yet unfulfilled. And now Isaac is approaching sixty, and they are still waiting to become parents.

As she waits, Rebekah undoubtedly wonders if God has forgotten her, not realizing that her years of barrenness are a part of His greater purpose. Kent Hughes explains,

> God was teaching his people that the promised blessing through the chosen seed of Abraham could not be accomplished by mere human effort. This is how it had been for Sarah. This is how it would be for her daughters-in-law Rachel and Leah. And later it would be the same for the mother of Samson and for Hannah, the mother of Samuel. And ultimately the promise would culminate with Elizabeth, the mother of John the Baptist and (in a class by herself) Mary, the mother of our Lord. [6]

Waiting seasons are not uncommon with God.

3. Think back on a season when you were waiting on God. What did you learn during that time?

Much to Isaac's credit, he does not try to help God out, like Abraham and Sarah did when they decided to use Hagar as a surrogate.

4. What does Isaac do in response to Rebekah's barrenness? (v. 21)

The word used for "prayed" in verse 21 is the same word used in Exodus to describe Moses' entreaty of God to remove the plagues from Egypt. Isaac intercedes on behalf of his wife with passion. And he keeps on praying for years, believing the covenant promise that God had given to his father. Derek Kidner notes, "God's way of prefacing an exceptional work with exceptional difficulties was often to take this form: men such as Joseph, Samson, and Samuel came into the world only after sorrow and prayer." [7] And then, what joy, when "the effectual fervent prayer of a righteous man availeth much" (James 5:16b, KJV), and Rebekah becomes pregnant!

But it is not long before Rebekah's joy begins to fade, as it feels like her womb has become a battlefield. Perplexed and in pain, she seeks the Lord for an answer.

5. What does God reveal to Rebekah about her sons? (v. 23)

Not only does the struggle in her womb foreshadow the lifelong relationship between her twins, but in His sovereignty, God has chosen the secondborn rather than the firstborn to be the heir of the promise. As Paul tells us in Romans 9:10-12,

> And not only this, but there was Rebekah also, when she had conceived twins by one man, our father Isaac; for though the twins were not yet born and had not done anything good or bad, so that God's purpose according to His choice would stand, not because of works but because of Him who calls, it was said to her, "The older will serve the younger."

Even though it is contrary to the cultural norms of the day, God has made His choice, and He doesn't make mistakes.

When the time comes for Rebekah to give birth to her twins, the first boy born is red-headed and hairy all over. The baby's red hair, uncommon in the Middle East, would have astounded his parents, but not quite as much as his hairy body. Isaac and Rebekah name their firstborn Esau, a name believed to be derived from an Arabic word meaning "hairy." As the second boy is born, he is holding on to his brother's heel as if to pull him back. They name him Jacob, which comes from the Hebrew verb that means "to follow at the heel," "to supplant," [8] and would later become a nickname meaning "to trick," or "to deceive." [9] In Jewish culture, a child's name is the beginning of a life story and is considered to have some prophetic significance. Given that, it would seem like Isaac and Rebekah might have been able to come up with better names than Hairy and the Heel-grabber. But alas, those are the names they choose. And as their stories continue, we will see that the boys will live up to their names.

Read Genesis 25:27-34.

As the twins grow up, they are polar opposites. Esau is a tough and rugged outdoorsman. A man's man who likes to hunt. Jacob, on the other hand, is a quiet man, a thinker, who prefers to stay around the tent. By the time the boys are young adults, they have become two very different individuals with very different values.

Moreover, the customs of their culture and the dysfunction of their family have created an unhealthy tension and competition between the twins. Their ancient Middle Eastern culture vastly favors firstborn sons, recipients of the birthright, who will "one day inherit a double portion of the estate, receive a special spoken blessing from his father, and run the family business." [10] In the times they live, everything is stacked in Esau's favor. Although Isaac and Rebekah cannot level the playing field fashioned by cultural traditions, they can give equal love and attention to their sons within the framework of their family. But sadly, making matters worse and playing favorites, "Isaac loved Esau because he had a taste for game, but Rebekah loved Jacob" (v. 28). Can't you imagine how Jacob felt when Esau came home with a deer or gazelle slung over his shoulder, and he heard his father brag on his brother's amazing hunting skills? If only he could hear similar words of affirmation from his father. But instead, he hears "Esau did this" and "Esau did that." Feelings of inferiority and shame kick in. Granted, Jacob has his mother's favor. But she cannot give him the inheritance and blessing he desires.

Outwardly, it appears to be a foregone conclusion which brother will serve the other. That is until Jacob sees an opportunity and seizes it. Matthew Henry calls what happens next "the most important meal since Eve ate the forbidden fruit." [11]

6. What does Esau exchange his birthright for? (vv. 29-34)

Instant gratification ("a swallow of that red stuff") is more important to Esau than his future, so he trades his entire future for a bowl of soup! Esau is consumed by his physical appetite. He is not really about to die. He is just hungry and tired. But his habit of giving in to immediate gratification causes him to exaggerate his hunger into a life-threatening situation.

7. What are some modern-day examples of the desire for instant gratification?

8. What are some ways that we can protect ourselves from being controlled by our physical appetites or desires?

Esau's birthright entitles him to great material wealth and leadership of the family after the death of Isaac, but there is something even greater. Think back on God's promise to Abraham in Genesis 12:1-3. This particular birthright includes the covenant blessing that God had promised to Abraham and Isaac. John Phillips explores the eternal consequences of Esau's trade:

> It all happened so suddenly. A few hasty words, but "out of the abundance of the heart, the mouth speaketh," so those few hasty words exposed the utter darkness of Esau's soul. A few hasty words, but they showed that the root of the matter was not in him at all; he was an unregenerate, ungodly, unspiritual man, a man ruled by appetite, a man who exemplified everything that the Bible means when it speaks of "the flesh." [12]

The patriarchal blessing means nothing to Esau. He lives for earthly things, not eternal things. As Paul writes in 1 Corinthians 2:14, "a natural man does not accept the things of the Spirit of God, for they are foolishness to him; and he cannot understand them, because they are spiritually appraised." Motivated solely by his flesh, Esau seals his fate. Although he will officially lose his birthright later, this is the moment when he gives into his carnal appetite and heads down the road of no return.

But what about Isaac, Rebekah, and Jacob's part in this episode? Does God's sovereign choice of Jacob over Esau excuse their actions? Wiersbe answers this often-debated question:

> The fact that God had already determined to give the covenant blessings to Jacob didn't absolve anybody in the family from their obligation to the Lord. They were all responsible for their actions, because divine sovereignty doesn't destroy human responsibility. In fact, knowing that we're the chosen of God means we have a greater responsibility to do His will. [13]

As the family story continues, we will see that God always holds His own responsible for their actions.

One quick side note before we move on. Did you catch Esau's nickname in verse 30? As Moses is writing, he wants to remind the people of God that the Edomites, enemies of Israel, are descendants of Esau. In Numbers 20, after the Israelites left Egypt, Moses requested that the king of Edom give them permission to pass through his land. But the king replied, "You shall not pass through us, or I will come out with the sword against you" (Numbers 20:18). And throughout the centuries that followed, there was enmity between Edom and Israel.

It's hard to understand why Esau would make such a foolish trade, isn't it? As Jesus said in Mark 8:36, "For what does it profit a man to gain the whole world, and forfeit his soul?" But how often do we do the same thing? We choose to indulge our flesh, and in doing so, scorn God's grace, and treat His Son's sacrifice on our behalf with contempt.

In short, we despise our own birthright.

Dear Child of God – "There is a fountain filled with blood drawn from Immanuel's veins; And sinners, plunged beneath that flood, lose all their guilty stains." [14] You are in the bloodline of the King! That is your birthright. You have access to everything your Father owns. It is your blessing. It. Is. Yours.

Act like an heir. Because you are.

**Act like an heir.
Because you are.**

day two

Genesis 26:1-35

If we were to watch a movie trailer of Genesis 26 that catches the highlights of each scene, we would find ourselves asking, "Haven't I seen this movie before?" As we dig into this chapter, over and over we will see circumstances and behaviors that will seem like they are repeats from the life of Abraham, only this time, played out in the life of his son, Isaac. In fact, as if to draw our attention to these similarities, Moses mentions Abraham eight times in the thirty-five verses. Wiersbe writes, "In one form or another each new generation must experience the same tests as previous generations." [15] But while the tests may be the same, each successive generation has the opportunity to break cyclic behaviors and generational sin. Today, we will view three scenes in the life of Isaac. Will he keep repeating the sin patterns in his family? Or will he forge a new way? Let's find out!

Scene I

Read Genesis 26:1-11.

1. What three events occur in Isaac's life that are similar to Abraham's account? (Look back at Genesis 12:1-13:4 to jog your memory.)

Given the arid conditions in Canaan, the possibility of a famine was a continual threat for those who lived there. One year, one planting season, without rain, and many would pack up their tents to move to greener pastures. It happened with Abraham. And now it happens with Isaac.

Isaac and Rebekah are likely living in Beer-lahai-roi (25:11) when this famine occurs. The son of the promise feels the weight of responsibility for his dependents. So just like his father did a century earlier, he loads up the camels and sets his course toward Egypt. Undoubtedly, Isaac has heard the family stories about the disastrous events his parents encountered in Egypt. Perhaps he thinks he will be able to learn from their mistakes and act differently. Or perhaps he just isn't thinking (and he certainly isn't praying), and he just wants the quickest way out of a bad situation. At any rate, his first inclination is to ask, "How can I get out of this?" instead of "What can I get out of this?" [16] Like father, like son, like us. Ouch!

But before heading out of Canaan, Isaac decides to head about 75 miles northeast to Gerar to see if he can get help from Abimelech, the king of the Philistines.

2. What happens when Isaac gets to Gerar? (v. 2)

3. What does God explicitly tell Isaac not to do? (v. 2)

God follows His prohibition to Isaac by confirming the promise He had given to Abraham. Seven times, as He speaks to Isaac, He affirms "His sovereign will in the matter and [pledges] Himself to be to Isaac all that He had been to Abraham." [17] Phillips points out that when God repeats the Abrahamic covenant to Isaac,

> God's Word came through in the crisis hour as remarkably relevant and up to date. Five times in that affirmation, Abraham's obedience was emphasized as a means of encouraging Isaac to trust and obey. Isaac's attention thus turned away from the situation in which he found himself and regarding which he was about to make a wrong move, and it was directed instead to the Word of God. [18]

May we take note of what Isaac does, and do the same!

To his credit, Isaac obeys God and does not leave Canaan. It seems as if the son will not repeat the father's mistake. Way to go, Isaac! Sort of.

4. As the rest of Scene I unfolds, what generational sin do we see that has been passed from Abraham to Isaac? (vv. 7-11)

Scholars differ on the opinion as to whether this is the same Abimelech that Abraham tried to deceive. But regardless, how sorry it is for a pagan king to call out a believer for their conduct. And shame on Isaac for placing his wife in the same dangerous situation that his father had put his mother!

Scene II

Read Genesis 26:12-22.

As Isaac's story moves on, God keeps the promise He made to Isaac and blesses him, even in the middle of a desperate famine. A one hundredfold increase during optimal weather conditions is rare, but in the midst of a famine, it is unheard of. But that is what happens when the favor of God rests upon a person. Even a person who lies and deceives? Yes, as Wiersbe explains:

> How could God bless somebody who claimed to be a believer and yet deliberately lied to his unbelieving neighbors? Because God is always faithful to His covenant and keeps His promises (2 Timothy 2:11-13), and the only condition attached to His promise is that Isaac remain in the land and not go to Egypt. [19]

5. Out of jealousy over Isaac's prosperity, what do the Philistines do? (v. 15)

Water is a precious commodity in the Middle East. And during a famine, it is even more valuable. In spite of the pact between Abimelech and Abraham regarding wells (Genesis 21:22-34), this generation of Philistines neither respect Abraham nor fear God. So, to alleviate a full-blown crisis on his watch, Abimelech tells Isaac to leave the area. Subsequently, Isaac moves from Gerar to the Gerar Valley and begins to excavate the wells that his father had dug decades earlier. When the wells are reestablished, Isaac gives them their original names as a means of affirming his property rights.

6. What happens next? (vv. 18-21)

When Isaac's servants dig a new well and discover a spring flowing with fresh water, the conflict between the Philistine herdsmen and Isaac's shepherds reignites and the locals take possession of the well. Isaac names this well, *Esek*, (contention). And then they dig another well and the herdsmen quarrel again. Isaac names this second well *Sitnah* (hatred, hostility). Isaac then moves further away and digs a third well and calls it *Rehoboth* (room), "at last the Lord has made room for us and we will be fruitful in the land" (v. 22). [20]

At peace, finally, Isaac moves to Beersheba where Abraham had lived for many years. On the night he arrives in Beersheba, God appears to Isaac once again.

7. What does God promise to Isaac and how does Isaac respond? (vv. 24-25)

Earlier when God appeared to Isaac in Gerar, His promise was in the future tense, "I will be with you and bless you" (26:3). This time, God promises His presence in the present tense, "I am with you" (26:24). Undoubtedly, Isaac believes that God is with him because he calls upon the name of the Lord, builds an altar, and worships the Lord (echoing what Abraham did when he entered the Promised Land). Isaac then puts down his tent stakes in Beersheba and digs another well. (Don't miss the repeated blessing of water God gives to Isaac during a time of famine.) Isaac is wealthy and could have afforded to build a beautiful home; instead he pitches his tent like his father, identifying him as "an alien in the land of promise" (Hebrews 11:9).

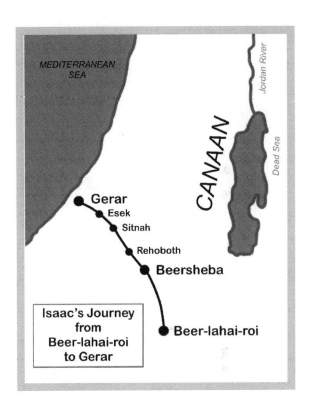

Isaac's Journey from Beer-lahai-roi to Gerar

Scene III

Right after the powerful meeting Isaac has with God, the Philistines show up. Again. But this time, they are singing a different tune. The king, one of his advisors, and the commander of the army encounter a stronger Isaac, one whose faith has been strengthened by the Lord. When Isaac boldly confronts the Philistine contingent, they quickly assert that they are only there to make a treaty with him. In spite of his earlier deception, the Philistines have been impressed by Isaac's conduct during the conflict over the wells, and they acknowledge the Lord's blessing on his life. To ratify the treaty, Isaac hosts a feast, "for in that culture, to eat with others was to forge strong links of friendship and mutual support." [21]

And then Scene III closes with the discovery of yet another well. The story that began with drought and famine ends with an abundance of water. Again, we see the grace of the sovereign God of the universe on majestic display!

A Quick Epilogue

While Isaac has established peace with his neighbors, there is a war brewing at home with his oldest son and his two (yes, not one, but two) heathen wives. More will be said about them later. But suffice it to say, Esau breaks his parents' hearts when he marries two unbelievers.

The story that began with drought and famine ends with an abundance of water.

One Last Thought

As you walked through this chapter in Isaac's story today, were you reminded of ways that you are like your parents? Or perhaps, because of the grace of God, ways that you are no longer like your parents? Peter reminds us, "For you know that God paid a ransom to save you from the empty life you inherited from your ancestors. And it was not paid with mere gold or silver, which lose their value. It was the precious blood of Christ, the sinless, spotless Lamb of God" (1 Peter 1:18-19, NLT). Much too high of a price has been paid for you to continue to live in the hand-me-downs of generational sin. Ask God to reveal any area to you that you need to repent of and determine that by the grace of God, right now, today, this (whatever your "this" is) ends with you.

If they confess their iniquity and the iniquity of their forefathers, in their unfaithfulness which they committed against Me, and also in their acting with hostility against Me – I also was acting with hostility against them, to bring them into the land of their enemies – or if their uncircumcised heart becomes humbled so that they then make amends for their iniquity, then I will remember My covenant with Jacob, and I will remember also My covenant with Isaac, and My covenant with Abraham as well, and I will remember the land.
Leviticus 26:40-42

"No weapon that is formed against you will prosper; And every tongue that accuses you in judgment you will condemn. This is the heritage of the servants of the Lord, And their vindication is from Me," declares the Lord.
Isaiah 54:17

And you will know the truth, and the truth will make you free.
John 8:32

day three

Genesis 27:1-29

The simplest definition of dysfunctional is "not functioning properly."[22] Synonyms for the term include flawed, broken, debilitated, defective, deteriorated, maladjusted, sick, and wounded. Every one of these words could be used interchangeably to describe three generations of family dysfunction in the Abraham – Isaac – Jacob family tree. As we come to Genesis 27, the family strain is reaching an all-time high.

Just to take a quick trip down dysfunctional memory lane, do you remember when:

- Abraham lied about Sarah being his sister?

- Abraham slept with Sarah's maidservant, Hagar?

- Abraham lied about Sarah being his sister again?

- Sarah was so mean to Hagar when she was pregnant that the expectant mother ran away?

- Abraham made Hagar and Ishmael leave after Sarah caught Ishmael making fun of Isaac?

- Isaac lied about Rebekah being his sister?

- Isaac and Rebekah chose favorites and created an epic sibling rivalry?

- Esau sold his birthright for a bowl of soup?

While up to this point the family unit has certainly not functioned properly, at least the nuclear family has managed to stay together. But that will soon change.

Let me preface this next very sad chapter in the Isaac, Rebekah, Jacob, and Esau saga by making three observations.

1. There are no spiritual heroes in this narrative. All four characters behave sinfully.

2. The four are never together at the same time to address the patterns of interpersonal deception and barriers of separation that have come between them and are on the verge of exploding.

3. The situation has not occurred overnight. Resentments and rivalries have been going on for years.

Let's examine each character and the role they play as the family unit is literally hanging on by a thread. We'll begin with the head of the home, Isaac.

Isaac

Read Genesis 27:1-4.

The Isaac we see here is not the once obedient unto death young man at Mount Moriah. The Isaac we see here is not the man who prayed for years that God would allow Rebekah to get pregnant. The Isaac we see here is not the patient well digger who was respected for his relationship with God by the unbelieving Philistines. No, the Isaac we see here is a man who has lost his spiritual edge. At some point in his walk with the Lord, he began to coast. And coasting only takes you one way – downhill.

As the story begins, Isaac is convinced that he is about to die. He is losing his eyesight and has become dependent upon his family. Scholars have estimated his age to be 137 at this time, the same age that his brother Ishmael died (25:17). [23] So, perhaps it is understandable why he wants to set his affairs in order. In reality, he is only heading into his fourth quarter; he will live another 43 years and die at the ripe old age of 180 (35:28). Sadly, Isaac's thoughts are full of death when he has so much of life left to live.

1. What does Isaac request from Esau and why? (vv. 3-4)

Isaac's motives are clear. As he sends Esau out to hunt for game, he is placing his son in the position of the firstborn, the provider for the family. Once Esau returns and prepares the meal, Issac plans to give him the blessing as the firstborn.

2. What is wrong with Isaac's plan? (Look back at Genesis 25:23.)

The patriarchal blessing is the greatest thing Isaac has to bequeath. This blessing is not just about material wealth. It is not just about becoming the head of the family. This blessing is "the right to stand in direct line as an ancestor of the coming Christ." [24] And it was not up to Isaac who would receive the blessing. God had already chosen Jacob over Esau. But Isaac doesn't care. In utter defiance of the revealed will of God, he wants the blessing to go to his favorite son and devises what he thinks is a secret plan to make that happen.

And his plan might have worked, except he has forgotten how thin the walls in his tent are and he doesn't realize that Rebekah is listening to every detail of his scheme.

Rebekah

3. Based upon what you already know about Rebekah, what words would you use to describe her?

Read Genesis 27:5-10.

Not to be outsmarted by her aging husband, Rebekah hatches her own equally manipulative scheme. (This family really is next-level dysfunctional!)

4. What are the basics of Rebekah's plot? (vv. 8-10)

As Sir Walter Scott wrote in his poem, "Marmion": "Oh what a tangled web we weave when first we practice to deceive." [25] Rebekah knows that Jacob is the one God has chosen to receive the covenant blessing. But rather than trust Him to bring about what He has promised, she takes matters into her own hands. Undoubtedly, she has "assured herself that 'Scripture' was on her side." [26] Phillips casts a wide net and points out that "it is amazing how proficient we are at finding proof texts that support our wayward desires." [27]

5. If you could have inserted yourself into this story, what verses would you have shared with Rebekah to let her know her deceptive plan does not line up with God's Word? (Old Testament and/or New Testament verses)

As Rebekah conspires with Jacob, she is pretty sure she has thought through every little detail of her plot. She knows her husband well, and is aware that the way to his heart is through his stomach. Now, she and Jacob just have to put the plan into action. Let's see what happens next when the Heel-grabber enters the story.

Jacob

Read Genesis 27:11-29.

6. What concern does Jacob raise about Rebekah's plan? (vv. 11-12)

Jacob has no moral qualms about his role. He doesn't mind deceiving; he just doesn't want to be known as a deceiver. Because, let's face it, Hairy is really, really, hairy, and Jacob is not. The Heel-grabber doesn't want to get caught trying to grab his brother's blessing and end up being cursed instead of blessed. But in true Rebekah fashion, his mother basically tells Jacob to just do what she says and let her take care of the rest.

Two goats later, the delicious smell of stew is wafting throughout the tent, Jacob is wearing Esau's best clothes, and he has goat skins tied around his arms and neck. The scene would be hilarious if it were not so tragic. Hughes calls our attention to the "deeper absurdity here—the mother and son's belief that God would not be able to accomplish His own purposes without their help. Mother and son believed that what they were doing helped God's revealed will along, and therefore their deceitful ways were justified." [28] Apparently, the enemy of their souls has really conned these two into believing that God needs their help, and that their sinful actions are fine and good as long as they are aiding His work.

So, convinced that the ends justify the means, Jacob picks up a mouthwatering bowl of goat stew, and pulls the trigger on their plan.

7. Write down the six lies that Jacob tells in verses 18-27.

Three lies are in the first sentence right out of his mouth! And then the fourth when he tries to pass off goat as "game" (venison). With the fifth lie, he adds the name of the Lord in an effort to make his deceit more acceptable. And his sixth lie is a repeat and reassurance to his father, who senses that something is wrong, but can't quite put his finger on exactly what it is.

Finally persuaded that the son with him must be Esau, Isaac gives Jacob a beautiful blessing, bestowing upon him "unlimited prosperity and power, the fatness of the earth, sovereignty over the nations, lordship over his brethren, [and] divine protection." [29]

This drama is not yet over. Tomorrow we will meet the fourth and final character in this saga as the family train finally goes off the rails.

But today, we close with this – even in the midst of lies, even in the throes of deception, God demonstrates His sovereignty. His will is accomplished as Jacob now officially receives the blessing of the firstborn from his father. Not that the deception is justified, but God is showing that He is able to use the sinful weakness of men to achieve His purposes.

Nothing in all the vast universe can come to pass otherwise than God has eternally purposed.
Here is a foundation of faith. Here is a resting place for the intellect.
Here is an anchor for the soul, both sure and steadfast. It is not blind fate,
unbridled evil, man or devil, but the Lord Almighty who is ruling the world, ruling
it according to His own good pleasure and for His own eternal glory. [30]
~ A.W. Pink

day four

Genesis 27:30 - 28:9

Let's pick back up where we left off yesterday. As Jacob scurries out of the room, he can hardly contain his excitement. His lies have worked! He has outwitted Esau – again. Once spoken, the blessing is a legal contract that cannot be revoked. But neither can the fallout that is about to happen be avoided.

As one man has said, "A little lie is like a little pregnancy – it doesn't take long before everyone knows."[31] And it doesn't take long at all for Jacob's little lies to be made public. Right after the Heel-grabber leaves his father, Esau returns from his hunt. And almost immediately, Isaac and Esau realize that they have been duped.

Read Genesis 27:30-40.

1. How does Isaac respond when he finds out that he has been deceived? (v. 33)

Like a convulsing earthquake, the realization that his lies have caught up with him tears through Isaac's entire body, and he is literally shaken to his core. He quakes as the awareness that Almighty God has overruled his deceitful plan settles upon his soul. Donald Grey Barnhouse makes this perceptive observation:

> Before a great work of grace, there must be a great earthquake. Isaac had put his personal love of Esau ahead of the will of God. Down came his idol, and the edifice of willful love collapsed before the shaking power that took hold of him. The arrogant pride which had slyly planned to thwart God toppled to the ground, broken beyond repair. When Isaac trembled exceedingly, all his desires were shattered.[32]

In essence, Isaac admits his defeat as he concludes, "Yes, and he shall be blessed" (v. 33).

Esau

When Esau initially sees his father's trembling reaction, he must wonder what is wrong. But then, as he processes Isaac's words, the full weight of what has happened while he was out hunting hits him.

2. What is Esau's response to the loss of the blessing? (vv. 34-36)

While Esau accurately portrays the character of his brother, he can only blame himself. It is not true, as Esau bemoans, that Jacob "took" his birthright. Esau gave it away. And why? Because he despised it. The ultimate culpability lies with Esau as Hebrews 12:15-17 makes clear:

> Look after each other so that none of you fails to receive the grace of God. Watch out that no poisonous root of bitterness grows up to trouble you, corrupting many. Make sure that no one is immoral or godless like Esau, who traded his birthright as the firstborn son for a single meal. You know that afterward, when he wanted his father's blessing, he was rejected. It was too late for repentance, even though he begged with bitter tears (NLT).

Wiersbe walks us through the Hebrews commentary on Esau, giving us insight into the older son's spiritual condition:

> Esau tried to repent, but his own heart was too hard, and he couldn't change his father's mind. Esau's tears were not tears of repentance for being an ungodly man; they were tears of regret because he had lost the covenant blessing. Esau wanted the blessing, but he didn't want to be the kind of man whom God could bless! We may forget our decisions, but our decisions don't forget us. [33]

Don't let Esau's tears make you feel sorry for him. Much like a toddler, he is just crying because he didn't get what he wanted. Wailing, he begs his father for a blessing.

3. Compare the blessing Isaac gives to Esau (vv. 39-40) with the blessing he gave to Jacob (vv. 27-29).

What a difference! In fact, the blessing Esau receives sounds more like an anti-blessing, doesn't it? There is nothing of eternal value in Isaac's blessing for his oldest son. Esau and his descendants, the Edomites, will not live under "dew" and "fatness" but "away" from those blessings of Heaven. Instead of ruling, they will live by the sword and be subservient to Israel. Wiersbe explains how this "blessing" came to pass historically:

> The Edomites who descended from Esau (Edom) built their nation at Mount Seir (36:6-8) at the southern end of the Dead Sea and were constant enemies of the Jews. During David's reign, the Edomites were subject to Israel, but when Joram was king of Judah, the Edomites rebelled and won their freedom (2 Kings 8:20-22). [34]

But clearly, the "blessing" Esau receives from Isaac is not what he wants to hear.

Read Genesis 27:41-46.

4. How does Esau "console" himself after he loses the firstborn blessing? (vv. 41-42)

Do you know what the modern-day term is for someone who finds comfort and pleasure at the thought of killing someone? A psychopath. Think Ted Bundy or Charles Manson. Or Esau.

And much like a psychopath, Esau obviously can't keep his homicidal thoughts to himself, because Rebekah finds out.

5. When Rebekah hears about what Esau is plotting, what plan does she devise to protect Jacob? (vv. 43-45)

Surely Esau will cool off in a few days, she reasons, and Jacob can return home.

6. How does Rebekah get Isaac to agree to send Jacob to visit her brother? (v. 46)

Rebekah's suggestion that Jacob might end up marrying a Hittite woman (like their other two daughters-in-law who have made their lives miserable) works. Actually, it works so well, that Isaac embraces the idea as his own and calls Jacob in for a father-son talk.

Read Genesis 28:1-4.

Apparently, the recent events have frightened Isaac "entirely out of his carnality" [35] and he finally assumes his patriarchal role as he gives direction to Jacob about his future. First, Isaac speaks to Jacob as a parent.

7. What instruction does Isaac give to Jacob? (vv. 1-2)

Given that most scholars believe that Jacob is in his seventies at this time, [36] it is interesting that this is the first time Isaac has talked with him about marriage or the fact that he should not marry an unbeliever. None too soon for Jacob, but decades late for Esau.

Next, Isaac speaks to his son as a patriarch and blesses Jacob again. When Isaac blessed Jacob in Genesis 27:27-28, he thought he was blessing Esau. This time, he knows that he is blessing Jacob

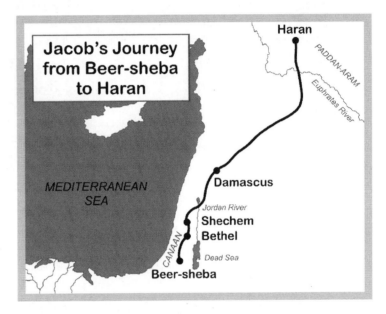

and he adds "the blessing of Abraham" as he conveys the covenant blessings to him. Then Isaac sends Jacob away to Rebekah's brother, some five hundred miles away to Haran in the land of Paddan-aram.

If this map looks familiar, it is because Jacob is basically backtracking his grandfather Abraham's trip into Canaan as he exits it.

As Jacob bids his parents farewell and heads north, Esau has taken notice of his father's words. Phillips explains,

> Esau took note of one fact. Isaac had sent Jacob away, not because he was afraid of reprisals Esau might institute, for with God's blessing resting on Jacob, there was nothing Esau could do to harm him. He had sent him away because of his fear of the women of Canaan. The wheels began to turn in Esau's carnal mind. *So that's why father refused to give me the blessing,* he thought. *He's put out because I did not marry a believer.* [37]

8. Thinking he can get back in Isaac's good graces, what does Esau do? (v. 9)

Jacob is headed off to marry one uncle's daughter, so Esau decides to marry his other uncle's daughter. Now he has married into Uncle Ishmael's family and has three wives. By no means, the recipe for a happy family!

This sad saga has no heroes.

- Not Isaac. He bowed up against the will of God. And lost.

- Not Rebekah. She wanted her favorite son to be sure to receive the blessing. He did, but she lost. It will be a long twenty years before Jacob returns home and by that time, Rebekah will have died. She will never see her preferred son again.

- Not Esau. He despised the promise and sold his birthright. Then, he spiraled into an angry, bitter man who consoled himself by plotting his brother's murder.

- Not Jacob. The deceiver and manipulator got what he wanted, but he has no idea how tough his life is about to get.

Hughes summarizes the root of the family issue:

> Everyone in the family sought the blessings of God without bending the knee to God. This little family was fraught with ambition, jealousy, envy, lying, deceit, coveting, malice, manipulation, stubbornness, and stupidity. And everyone lost. [38]

9. How is Galatians 6:7-8 a fitting commentary on Isaac and his family?

At the beginning of Genesis, God created a perfect family system. But when sin entered the world, the family became one of Satan's prime targets. In fact, the very first attack of Satan was on the family (Genesis 3:1-6). And that attack which resulted in the fall of man had widespread consequences that are still being felt by families in the twenty-first century. Dysfunction – family malfunction – is the result of sin. Every family has some extent of dysfunction because every member of every family is a sinner. But there is hope.

As dysfunctional as the Abraham – Isaac – Jacob family tree is, it is also the story of how mankind's sin is covered by the unmerited, unfailing grace of God. And He has not changed. The God of Abraham, Isaac, and Jacob offers mercy in lavish abundance on all who believe. He offers hope for every person, for every family.

Through Christ Jesus, God has blessed the Gentiles with the same blessing He promised to Abraham, so that we who are believers might receive the promised Holy Spirit through faith.
Galatians 3:14, NLT

day five

The Blessing of God's Smile

The LORD bless you, and keep you;
The LORD make His face shine on you, and be gracious to you;
The LORD lift up His countenance on you, and give you peace.
Numbers 6:24-26

In 1979, during the excavation of a Jewish burial chamber near the Old City of Jerusalem, archaeologists discovered two tiny silver scrolls, no larger than the diameter of a quarter. The scrolls, originally worn as amulets around the neck, are believed to be the oldest biblical text in existence, dating back to around 600 B.C. When the scrolls were unrolled, researchers discovered that the Hebrew text on the amulets was the priestly blessing, Numbers 6:24-26. These ancient amulets were worn according to the instructions given to the Israelites in Deuteronomy 6:6-9,

> These commandments that I give you today are to be on your hearts. Impress them on your children. Talk about them when you sit at home and when you walk along the road, when you lie down and when you get up. Tie them as symbols on your hands and bind them on your foreheads. Write them on the doorframes of your houses and on your gates (NIV).

These small scrolls were worn as a reminder of the blessing of God that He had taught to Israel as they were preparing to move into the Promised Land. The words of this text are known as the priestly or Aaronic blessing, but this is not a blessing written by men. These are God's words.

1. How many times does God say the word "you" in this blessing? (Numbers 6:24-26)

The repeated "you" pronouns in this blessing are in the singular form, indicating this is an individual blessing, not a corporate blessing. [39] God wants to bless <u>you</u>.

2. Process that thought for a moment. God desires to bless you. How does that realization make you feel?

Let's walk through this blessing line-by-line, verse-by-verse, so that we can comprehend the magnitude of what it really means for us.

3. What are the first two words of each line in Numbers 6:24-26?

Three times, God's covenant name, *Yahweh* (the LORD in all caps), is repeated, emphasizing that He is the source of the blessing. Then each line follows with two verbs. The first line (v. 24) sums up the heart of this blessing, "The LORD *bless* you and *keep* you." Line two (v. 25) elaborates on the verb "bless" while line three (v. 26) develops the verb "keep." [40]

Bless – *The LORD make His face shine on you, and be gracious to you.*

The Hebrew word for bless, *barak*, means "to kneel down," as seen in Genesis 24:11 when Abraham's servant made his camels kneel down to be watered. Used figuratively in Numbers 6:24, it pictures God's movement toward us as He bends down to bless us. Now notice in 6:25 God's face as He seeks us out – it is shining. His face lights up when He looks at us. When we see a loved one and our faces light up, the emotion that shines through is joy. Similarly, God is joyful, He is happy when He is with us. Numbers 6:24 expresses the delight of God to be with us and can be paraphrased, "May you feel the joy of God's face shining on you because He is happy to be with you." [41] Do you know what happens when our faces light up? We smile. And when God's face lights up, He does the same.

So let me ask you, *Do you really believe that God is happy to be with you?* Or has the title of Jonathan Edwards' famous sermon, "Sinners in the Hands of an Angry God," influenced the way you think about the way God thinks about you? Before you label me a heretic, please hear me out. Edwards was a catalyst for revival in his time and left an amazing legacy. But I have to wonder about the lasting impact of his characterization of God:

> The God that holds you over the pit of Hell, much as one holds a spider, or some loathsome insect, over the fire, abhors you, and is dreadfully provoked; His wrath toward you burns like fire; He looks upon you as worthy of nothing else, but to be cast into the fire; He is of purer eyes than to bear to have you in his sight; you are ten thousand times so abominable in His eyes as the most hateful venomous serpent is in ours. [42]

Yes, we are all sinners, "for all have sinned and fall short of the glory of God" (Romans 3:23). However, there is a difference between how God views lost people and saved people. Edwards' depiction of God does apply, in part, to those who do not have a relationship with Christ. Before a person repents and believes in Jesus, he is the enemy of God (Colossians 1:21). Yet, even before that person comes to Christ, he is loved by God (Romans 5:8). Only God can love and hate perfectly. The person who rebelliously clings to his sin and refuses to repent will be judged by God (Revelation 20:15).

Child of God, God's thoughts toward you are love, and His desire is for you to know the blessing of His smile.

But Edwards' words do not apply to those who have a relationship with Christ. Why? Because of the cross – because of Jesus. Believers have been rescued "from the domain of darkness and transferred us to the Kingdom of His beloved Son, in Whom we have redemption, the forgiveness of sin" (Colossians 1:13-14). And even though God disciplines His children when they sin, He takes no delight in doing so. Child of God, God's thoughts toward you are love, and His desire is for you to know the blessing of His smile.

4. When you think about God and your relationship with Him, how do you view Him? As an angry God who is just waiting for you to mess up? Or as a loving Father bending His knee to get down in your face so that you can see His smile toward you?

Keep – *The LORD lift up His countenance on you, and give you peace.*

The picture of God keeping us is expanded in Numbers 6:25. Not only does God smile at us, but He also turns His face toward us, He takes notice of us. Psalm 121:7-8 expounds upon the ways God keeps His children:

> The Lord will <u>keep</u> you from all evil;
>
> He will <u>keep</u> your life.
>
> The Lord will <u>keep</u> your going out and your coming in from this time forth and forevermore. (ESV)

The blessing of God in Numbers 6:24-26 invokes the protection of God, which subsequently gifts us with "peace." This peace, this *shalom*, is not merely the absence of war; it is a life of wholeness, well-being, and flourishing. Succinctly stated, it is the blessed life.

Throughout our study this week, the tension in Jacob's life has been the problem of the unblessed life. Jacob has spent decades feeling that he is unblessed because Esau was born first. Discounting the Word God has already spoken, Jacob has swallowed the cultural belief that secondborn sons can't be fully blessed hook, line, and sinker. His lack of belief in what God has said has triggered issues that will go unresolved for years.

Alan Wright asks a pointed question for our consideration, "What cultural voice of condemnation attacks you most?" [43] He then goes on to identify reasons our culture tells you that you can't be blessed:

> *You aren't smart enough*
>
> *You didn't come from the right family*
>
> *You don't have enough money*
>
> *You have made too many mistakes*
>
> *You aren't pretty enough*
>
> *You don't know the right people.* [44]

Do any of those thoughts resonate with you? If so, you are listening to the wrong voice. Take heart and hear the voice of Truth. God is bending down, His smiling face beaming, to bless you.

> *The LORD bless you, and keep you;*
> *The LORD make His face shine on you, and be gracious to you;*
> *The LORD lift up His countenance on you, and give you peace.*
> Numbers 5:24-26

Blessed to Be a Blessing

As we have said throughout this study, God blesses us so that we can be a blessing. But you cannot give what you do not possess. You cannot bless others if you are choosing to believe the lie that you are not blessed.

This week:

- Write out Numbers 6:24-26 on five different cards and place those cards in places where you will be reminded of God's blessing on you repeatedly throughout your day.

- Begin and end every day by internalizing God's blessing in the form of thanksgiving back to Him. *Thank you, Lord for blessing and keeping me. How blessed I am for Your presence in my life! How grateful I am for Your smile! Your face is always toward me, guarding me and protecting me. I receive Your peace and acknowledge Your blessing upon me.*

Once the realization of God's blessing on your life saturates your heart, get ready to bless someone else. As Wright explains:

> Blessed people flourish by a power that transcends human talent or hard work. They have a mystical grace at work in their hearts that makes them effective and joyful. People who know they are blessed aren't struggling to prove their worth—they're confident of their value and sure they can make a difference in the world. That's why blessed people bless people. That's why blessed people don't feel helpless to help others. [45]

As you go throughout your week, listen to the narratives of the people around you. Undoubtedly, it will not take very long before you will identify someone who is having the Jacob struggle of the unblessed life. You will see it on his or her face. You will hear it in the person's self-deprecating words. Gently begin to speak words of truth and blessing into that person's life. You may even want to give them one of your cards with the words of Numbers 6:24-26 on it and share what God is teaching you about His blessing upon your life. It may take a few days, or even weeks, but be sure to pay attention as the power of the blessing begins to take hold in that person's life.

Other than God's work through prayer,
blessing is the most powerful tool for change in the world. [46]
~ Alan Wright

You are blessed to be a blessing!

eight

JACOB DECEIVES
Genesis 28:10-31:55

*Life isn't easy, and what life does to us depends a
great deal on what life finds in us.* [1]
~ Warren Wiersbe

Jacob is a homeless fugitive, heading out for Haran. As a result of stealing Esau's birthright, he is fleeing an angry brother and facing an unknown future. This week we will find that he has a life-changing encounter with God that will carry him through some tumultuous years. Even though he has just dedicated himself to the Lord, he will still face the consequences of his choices as he continues his journey to Paddan-aram. Walking through this lesson, we will see the biblical principle of reaping and sowing, but we will also see the heart of God, filled with mercy and grace, as He continues to work in the lives of His children.

These chapters are full of valuable life lessons that are often drowned out by the culture's messages of self-gratification and personal satisfaction.

We serve a God whose very heart is that of forgiveness, grace, mercy, redemption, and restoration.

Sin carries the weight of consequences – there is no escaping it – but we also serve a God whose very heart is that of forgiveness, grace, mercy, redemption, and restoration. And He calls us to exhibit these same characteristics as we follow Jesus Christ.

As we study the next several years in Jacob's life, I pray we will see this account as Warren Wiersbe does: "A contemporary story about all of us who are making important decisions on the road of life, decisions that determine character and destiny." [2]

While he is fleeing for his life, Jacob stops for a night in Bethel. [3] He is surely worn and weary, both from running away in fear and traveling what is believed to be about 40 miles. On a hillside scattered with rocks and boulders, Jacob makes his bed, using a stone for his pillow. As darkness descends and sleep finally comes, he is about to have an encounter with the Lord that will leave him clinging to the promises of God in the days and years to come.

Read Genesis 28:10-15.

Jacob sleeps. And has a dream.

1. What does he see in his dream? (v. 12)

2. What promises are given to Jacob in the dream? (vv. 13-15)

Reread verse 15. Do these words not wash over your heart and mind with such peace and comfort? Consider Jacob's frame of mind as he lays his head on his stone pillow to get some much-needed rest. Physical and emotional exhaustion. Fear. Anxiety. Remorse. Uncertainty. And his God – our God – comes to him as he rests, speaking His promises and presence over him when Jacob needs it the most.

Although Jacob has willingly participated in Rebekah's scheme (and would later face the consequences), the Lord does not rebuke him in this moment. Instead, He is watching over him, promising His presence and protection wherever Jacob goes.

Dear weary sister, lay down and rest. Let the same God of Jacob speak His promises over you and surround you with His presence. Regardless of your circumstance, He wants to do this in your life. Even if you, like Jacob, are running because of your own sin and mistakes, His Word is full of promises for you. His presence will surround you, hold you, and carry you through.

Read Genesis 28:16-19.

3. What does Jacob do when he wakes up? (vv. 18-19)

Tony Evans notes, "What had been a dark place became a sacred space. Nothing had changed in Jacob's circumstances. All that had changed was Jacob getting a fresh vision of God. And that transformed everything." [4]

4. Is there a time in your life where your circumstances did not necessarily change, but a fresh Word from God changed you?

Read Genesis 28:20-22.

5. What does Jacob do before he moves on from Bethel? (vv. 20-22)

Wiersbe says of this vow, "Jacob wasn't making a bargain with God; he was affirming his faith in God. Since God had promised to care for him, be with him, and bring him back home safely, then Jacob would affirm his faith in God and would seek to worship and honor Him alone." [5] As Psalm 46:7 tells us, "The LORD of hosts is with us; the God of Jacob is our refuge" (NKJV).

Jacob is fortified by the promises of God given to him at Bethel and continues his journey. As he arrives "in the land of the east" (Genesis 29:1), he comes upon a well. Shepherds, along with their flocks, are waiting for the appropriate time to water their sheep and goats.

Read Genesis 29:1-8.

6. What is the custom in watering the flocks? (v. 3)

The shepherds answer Jacob's questions about where they are from and specifics about Laban and his well-being.

7. What did they point out to him and how does he respond? (vv. 6-7)

Some commentators say Jacob wanted to meet Laban's daughter under proper circumstances, while others say that Jacob takes matters into his own hands and orchestrates the circumstances so that he can have Rachel's undivided attention. Either way, I like Wiersbe's observation, "We see the providence of God in this meeting. In the life of the trusting Christian, there are no accidents, only appointments." [6]

Read Genesis 29:9-14.

Jacob goes against the custom of watering the animals and moves the stone from the mouth of the well so he can water Laban's flock.

8. What does Jacob do next and how does Rachel respond? (vv. 11-12)

9. Upon receiving the news, what does Laban do? (vv. 13-14)

Read Genesis 29:15-30 to see how the plot thickens. Jacob has been with Laban for about a month now. Good ole Uncle Laban insists that Jacob be paid for his work and asks Jacob how much his wages should be. Before we move into the agreement between Jacob and Laban, we are given some details about these two daughters, Leah and Rachel.

10. What is said about Rachel and what is said about Leah? (vv. 16-17)

- Rachel -

- Leah -

Verses 18-20 tell us that Jacob falls in love with Rachel and is willing to work seven years to have her as his wife. Jacob and Laban agree on these terms and the time comes for Jacob to marry Rachel. Here we begin to see Jacob reaping what he has sown.

11. What happens the night of the wedding feast and how does Jacob react? (vv. 21-25)

The deceiver has now been deceived! The *Life Application Study Bible* says, "How natural it is for us to become upset at an injustice done to us while closing our eyes to the injustices we do to others. Sin has a way of coming back to haunt us." [7]

Oh, how careful we must be! We are so quickly and easily angered and offended when we are done wrong, but we often fail to recognize the wrongdoing we have done to others.

Read Genesis 29:26-30.

I love the remainder of today's text as we begin to see a change in Jacob's character. This points us to the redemptive heart of God. Yes, Jacob has reaped what he sowed, but he has also learned a lesson and sticks to his end of the bargain even though Laban was tricky and deceptive. Wiersbe observes, "Jacob was learning to submit to God's loving hand of discipline and was growing in faith and character." [8]

Inspect your heart today. Have you been unjust toward someone and need to make it right? Are you harboring unforgiveness or bitterness for a wrong committed against you? Do you have a heart that seeks revenge or one that seeks reconciliation?

Our actions, righteous or unrighteous, will always bear fruit in keeping with the roots. [9]
~ Tony Evans

day two

Genesis 29:31-35

Before we dive into today's text, I want to spend a moment looking at the heart of God. This account of Scripture gives us powerful truth that can be easily lost or forgotten as women.

First, in yesterday's lesson, we read about the physical differences between Leah and Rachel. One was perceived to be beautiful and the other was not. Rachel is described as having a "beautiful figure and a lovely face," while Leah is described as having "no sparkle in [her] eyes" (Genesis 29:17, NLT).

Our culture has always been, but now seems especially hyper-focused on physical beauty. At every turn, we see advertisements, products, and services that promise a more youthful, attractive appearance. We are bombarded with the latest fashion trends, what's hot and what's not, and called upon as women to dress in a way that is sexually appealing, carrying ourselves with boldness and confidence.

To be clear…I enjoy fashion trends and keeping up with the latest styles. I take care of my skin in hopes of keeping a youthful appearance as long as possible. I exercise and try to stay fit for the purposes of good health and staying attractive for my husband. Not one of these things is wrong in and of themselves; taking care of God's temple is keeping in line with Scripture. However, if it consumes us and takes priority over our inner beauty, if it matters more to be eye-catching to this world rather than favored by Almighty God, if it fuels our significance and worth more than resting in who we are as His children, it becomes sin.

I found Bob Deffinbaugh's observation on beauty to be poignant and powerful. Regardless of your age or stage in life, I encourage you to read this slowly and allow the truth of it to sink deep into your heart, drowning out the lies of the world that outward beauty is most important.

> Ladies, I realize that our society has placed a premium on glamour and beauty. I understand that much of your sense of self-worth is based upon your outward attractiveness and "sex appeal." However, that is wrong. Our ultimate worth is that estimation which comes from God. God was not impressed with Rachel's good looks. After all, He gave that to her in the first place. God looked upon the heart and blessed Leah. Her worth, while never fully realized by her husband, was great in the eyes of God. May all of us learn to be content with ourselves as God made us, and may we find our real worth in the realm of the spirit. [10]

Second, it can be easy for us to slip into a pit of insignificance and lack of worth when we feel we don't measure up. Comparison is such a tool of the enemy in the lives of women. He attacks our minds with the temptation to compare at every turn. And while much good can come from social media, I believe it is also one of the craftiest tools of the enemy when it comes to comparison. Please be careful in this arena as you post and peruse, operating in Holy Spirit wisdom and discernment.

In the days of Leah and Rachel, a woman's significance was greatly tied to her ability to bear children. The more children she had, the more significant she was. Otherwise, she was considered a disgrace.

Read Genesis 29:31-35.

1. What do we see immediately in verse 31 about our God?

The New Living Translation reads, "When the LORD saw…." Those words wash over my heart, soothing and comforting as I read them. Throughout Scripture, we find a God who sees the hearts of His people, meeting them right where they are. I do not have to be like you. You do not have to be like me. We do not have to have the same calling, the same ministry, the same family structure, the same house, car, or education. Our clothes and shoes can be different. Our hairstyles and cooking styles can vary one to another.

> **Throughout Scripture, we find a God who sees the hearts of His people, meeting them right where they are.**

Number of children, choice of school, hobbies, size of house, vacation spots…it can all look so different from woman to woman. We can get so caught up in these things and miss what matters most. Colossians 3:2 says, "Think about the things of Heaven, not the things of earth" (NLT).

God sees our heart. God cares most about what's inside and how we are living it out on the outside. It doesn't matter if you are doing His work in the latest trends or sporting a look from way back. It doesn't matter if you are ministering to others with your six children at your side or with one or none. What He desires is you walking through this life with your eyes fixed on Him, obeying His Word and sharing Jesus with a lost world.

Leah felt unloved by Jacob and, I'm certain, inferior to Rachel. But God saw her.

And God sees you. Maybe you feel unloved. Perhaps you feel "less than" or undesirable to those around you. First of all, that is not true. And second, even if it were, God loves you and yearns for you. You are "fearfully and wonderfully made" (Psalm 139:14), and God has a specific and good plan for your life (Jeremiah 29:11).

So, by the providential hand of God, Leah becomes pregnant and gives birth to several children.

2. Write out the names of Leah's children and the meaning of their names. (vv. 32-35)

As we close today, take a few moments to journal your thoughts on how God sees you.

- Has today's study shifted your focus in the area of outward beauty vs. inward beauty?

- Have you allowed comparison to affect how you view your significance and worth?

- How can you put into practice being more focused on your worth in the realm of the Spirit?

- How can you teach those coming behind you?

If the Bible makes no other point, it shouts this one: God loves us! All we need to do is respond, not try to earn what is freely offered. Live life fully, in the freedom of knowing you are loved. [11]
~ Life Application Study Bible

GOD judges persons differently than humans do. Men and women look at the face; GOD looks into the heart.
1 Samuel 16:7, MSG

day three

Genesis 30

We now come to Genesis 30, where we see Rachel responding to her circumstances. As noted yesterday, Rachel is feeling the cultural pressure of not having any children.

Read Genesis 30:1-13.

1. What emotion is Rachel experiencing and how does Jacob respond? (vv. 1-2)

Wiersbe's observations give us insight:

> That Jacob could become angry with his favorite wife shouldn't surprise us. Even the most loving couples have their occasional disagreements, and, after all, she was blaming him for something over which he had no control. But what Rachel needed wasn't a lecture on theology or gynecology. She needed the kind understanding of her husband and the encouragement that only his love could provide. [12]

2. What is Rachel's plan for conceiving a child? (vv. 3-8)

Doesn't that sound familiar? Remember Abraham and Sarah? The *Life Application Study Bible* notes, "Jacob would have been wise to refuse, even though this was an accepted custom of the day. The fact that a custom is socially acceptable does not mean it is wise or right. You will be spared much heartbreak if you look at the potential consequences, to you or others, of your actions." [13]

As you read this, do you not immediately think of our world today? Truly, nothing is new under the sun. We are bombarded with socially accepted norms; moreover, we as Christians are ridiculed and characterized as haters if we stand up against them. While we are called to speak the truth in love and show Christlike love to those with whom we disagree, we must stand firm on the truth of God's Word and not cave to what society constitutes as acceptable when it clearly contradicts the authority of Scripture.

3. What are some socially acceptable customs today that stand in opposition to the Bible?

4. What instruction do we see in Romans 12:2 and what is the result of our obedience to it?

5. Write out the names of Rachel's children through Bilhah (with the meanings of their names). (vv. 6-8)

The saga continues as Leah realizes she is no longer conceiving children. She, like Rachel, resorts to human effort to bring about her desires. She offers her servant, Zilpah, to Jacob, in hopes of producing more children for him.

6. List Leah's most recent children through Zilpah (with the meanings of their names). (vv. 10-13)

Like a modern-day soap opera, the sisters' manipulative schemes continue as they compete for Jacob's affection. Read Genesis 30:14-24.

7. What transpires with Reuben, Leah, and Rachel? (vv. 14-15)

The result of the mandrake exchange is more children for both women. Leah gives birth to sons, Isaachar and Zebulun, and daughter Dinah.

8. What does verse 22 tell us again about the Lord?

God's character cannot be overstated or overemphasized. With every turn of every page in Scripture, God's character is on display. Do not miss it. He remembers Rachel's plight and answers her prayer, in spite of her insistence to do things her own way. God, not the mandrakes, brings Joseph onto the scene, the very one God will use to save their family years from now.

We are so tempted to step in and interfere, are we not? Waiting on and trusting God can be difficult; however, the consequences of stepping into God's role can be painful, leading to long-term suffering for us and generations to come. Diane Miller writes,

> Basically, both Leah and Rachel had to learn the same lesson. Their sufficiency, their happiness could not come from their husband or even their children. Their jealousy, sibling rivalry, bitterness, envy over what they did not have, did not lead to happiness. Only when they saw, at times, that their source of true fulfillment was in Yahweh, the Lord and His blessings did they find peace. [14]

As we continue moving through Genesis 30, we see Jacob wanting to leave Laban after fulfilling his part of the bargain. He is ready to take his family and return to his homeland and be on his own. Laban, though, knows he has been blessed because of Jacob's presence and does not want him to leave. We see further trickery from both men.

9. Read Genesis 30:25-43 and summarize the arrangement between Jacob and Laban.

There are various explanations for this text, but most importantly, we see the providential hand of God supernaturally intervening to allow Jacob to prosper. Jacob simply needs to obey God. (This is based on a vision we will see later in Genesis 31.)

In *Answers in Genesis*, Troy Lacey explains, "We are not told in Scripture if God miraculously changed the genetic makeup of the flocks or whether he just divinely guided those with the genetic information for stripes, spots and/or mottling to outcompete the other animals. But either way, this was providentially directed." [15]

With every turn of every page in Scripture, God's character is on display.

Is there an area of your life that you need to lay down and entrust to the providential hand of God? If so, write it here and commit to laying it down and leaving it at His feet to work through it as He sees fit.

Life isn't easy, but if we submit to God's disciplines and let Him guide us in our decisions,
we can endure the difficulties triumphantly and develop the kind of character that glorifies God.
The God of Jacob never fails. [16]
~ Warren Wiersbe

Genesis 31

God leads us in the paths of righteousness if we're willing to follow. [17]
~ Warren Wiersbe

It is now time for Jacob to go back home. We read in Genesis 30:25 that Jacob had a desire to return home. And it seems that desire has not left his heart. Wiersbe says the Lord led Jacob "the same way He leads His people today: through the inner witness in the heart, the outward circumstances of life, and the truth of His Word." [18]

How vital in the life of a believer to be in tune with the heart of the Father as we evaluate our positions and consider our options! Not every desire of our heart or every circumstance is a clear directive from the Lord, but He often speaks in these ways. One thing we can be sure of is the trustworthiness of His Word. As we open the pages of Scripture and digest the truth therein, we can rest assured He will not mislead us.

Read Genesis 31:1-3.

1. What do we see about Jacob's circumstances (v. 1), the leading of his heart (v. 2), and the Word of the Lord (v. 3)?

Read Genesis 31:4-13.

Jacob calls to Leah and Rachel and explains his reasoning for wanting to leave. He shares with them the dream he had and how the angel of the Lord had spoken to him.

2. What does the angel of God say to Jacob and what does this teach us about the character of God? (vv. 12-13)

3. Reflect on a time when God vindicated you, moved on your behalf, or stood as your Defender and Waymaker (consider sharing with your small group).

Read Genesis 31:14-21.

After listening to Jacob, Leah and Rachel agree that Laban has treated them poorly and are content with Jacob's desire to leave. Jacob decides against facing Laban to be upfront and honest with him. Rather, he flees without a trace, before Laban even notices they are gone. Moreover, Rachel steals her father's household idols as they leave. In relation to this text, Wiersbe observes, "It isn't enough to know and do the will of God; we must also do His will in the way He wants it done, the way that will glorify Him the most." [19]

Jacob knows God's will in this situation as God has clearly told him to return home (v. 13), but he goes about it in the wrong manner, acting out of fear and unbelief. Rachel agrees with Jacob's plan to leave, but takes the idols, either out of fear of losing their protection or out of fear Laban will use them to find their location. Either way, she is fearful and faithless as well.

4. What does Colossians 3:15 teach us?

5. How can we, at times, be ruled by fear rather than peace?

Read Genesis 31:22-42.

After three days, Laban discovers that Jacob has fled. He gathers a group and is in hot pursuit. He catches up with Jacob and his family a week later, but is restrained in his response because of a dream the previous night.

6. In keeping with His unchanging character, what instruction does God give Laban in the dream? (v. 24)

Laban manipulated and attempted to control Jacob during their years together. But our faithful God promised to protect Jacob…and, as always, He keeps His promise.

Greg Brown compares Laban to the world and makes this insightful observation:

> Laban is a picture of the world. He lived for money and riches and was willing to deceive and hurt others in order to get them – including hurting his family. He had a form of religion – an awareness of God – but didn't follow him. The world does the same with us. It will offer us blessings, like wealth, popularity, or promotion, if we'll follow and turn away from God. The world aims to press and mold us into its image. When we conform – through adopting its language, thought-processes, and practices – the less we are able to test and approve God's will. Not only will we be unable to follow God, we won't even be able to discern his will. [20]

7. What are some ways we can be in the world yet be separate from it?

Jacob becomes very angry as Laban begins rummaging through their possessions in search of the stolen idols. It seems the buried feelings from years of deception and manipulation come to the surface, and Jacob lays out his frustration and anger.

In Genesis 31:38-42, Jacob recounts the underhandedness of Laban's actions over the years. He specifically recounts the ways Laban has unjustly treated him and how he has gone above and beyond, doing more than was expected of him, which resulted in Laban's wealth and success.

8. What does Jacob reaffirm about his God and how does this speak to you specifically? (v. 42)

The remainder of Genesis 31 is the truce we see form between Jacob and Laban. Many commentators point out that this is not a declaration of peace, but more a protection of one against the other, ensuring they will not cross boundaries and bring harm to each other. Laban's oath may have been more superstitious in nature, but Jacob's memorial shows his faith in the one true God. Although he has exhibited a weak faith at times, he ultimately knows the One in Whom he can wholly trust. God faithfully protects him in the midst of it all, despite his shortcomings, and reveals to him that He will never leave him or forsake him.

The same applies to us. God sees, defends, protects, vindicates, and blesses His children. Only trust Him.

Close out your time today by "setting up a monument" as Jacob did. Set aside time to commemorate God's faithfulness to you in a specific situation. Recount how He saw you when it seemed no one else did, how He defended, protected, and vindicated you. Record the ways He blessed you in the midst of a difficult time and drew your heart closer to His.

When our primary motive becomes trusting God, we suddenly discover there is nothing in the world that pleases Him more! Until you trust God, nothing you do will please God. Pleasing is not a means to our godliness. It's the fruit of our godliness, for it's the fruit of trust. Trusting is the foundation of pleasing God. [21]
~ John Lynch

day five

The Blessing of the Firstborn

The Son is the image of the invisible God, the firstborn over all creation.
Colossians 1:15, NIV

During ancient times, the firstborn was given rights and special privileges, as well as the best of the inheritance. We read many accounts in the Old Testament of the blessing of the firstborn. Israel is referred to as God's "firstborn" (Exodus 4:22) because it held a special place of privilege and blessing among the nations.

As we move to the New Testament, we see in Luke 2:7 that Mary "gave birth to her firstborn son." We see in Colossians 1:15 the supremacy of Christ declared, "The Son is the image of the invisible God, the firstborn over all creation" (NIV).

The blessing of the firstborn takes on a whole new, and quite powerful, meaning! Jesus Christ is the firstborn and we, as heirs with Him, receive the ultimate blessing of abundant and eternal life because of His death and resurrection.

Read Galatians 3:14.

1. Through Christ, what do we receive and how do we receive it?

Evans states, "Remember: God promised to bless all the nations (the Gentiles) through Abraham. This blessing – justification by faith – comes to the world through the seed, the descendant of Abraham: Jesus Christ." [22]

Because of what Jesus Christ has done for us on the cross, we, who have faith, receive the promise of the Holy Spirit (as stated in Galatians 3:14).

Evans goes on to say, "You cannot inherit, earn, or buy the Holy Spirit. You can only receive Him as a free gift from God through His Son. It is the Spirit's role to activate the perfect righteousness of Christ, Who has already fulfilled the law, in the life of a believer who lives by faith." [23]

On the heels of finishing up this week's writing, I was reading through Ephesians 1 in my quiet time early one morning. Moments later, my mom called. We had been talking the day before about the blessing of the firstborn. She shared this with me and it, coupled with my reading in Ephesians, made it all so clear.

For the last few years, my grandfather has been giving my mom a small portion of her inheritance, a little bit along the way. When he writes out the check, he notes "living inheritance" on the memo line. He is blessing her with some of her inheritance while she is still living on this earth. As his daughter, she is receiving a blessing now and a glimpse of what is to come. My mom, in turn, has done the same for her children.

Do you see the heart of our Heavenly Father in this earthly example? We have been given every spiritual blessing *now*. We lack nothing to live out this earthly journey of faith and obedience *now*. Yes, so much more awaits us on the other side of eternity…more than we can begin to comprehend. But He is blessing us *now*. He graciously and lovingly gives us bits of our inheritance as we read His Word, pray, walk, and talk with Him, lean into Him during times of pain and suffering, share His truth with others, and minister hope and healing in the name of Jesus. We don't have to wait until we get to Heaven to get what is already ours because of Jesus Christ!

Ephesians 1:3 says, "All praise to God, the Father of our Lord Jesus Christ, who has blessed us with *every spiritual blessing in the heavenly realms* because we are united with Christ" (NLT, emphasis mine). Not some, not few…but *every* spiritual blessing. He is not withholding anything from us. He is not keeping it all stored up somewhere in Heaven. He has given it to us, just as a firstborn receives his right and inheritance.

The *Life Application Study Bible* notes, "In Christ, we have all the benefits of knowing God – being chosen for salvation, being adopted as His children, forgiveness, insight, the gifts of the Spirit, power to do God's will, the hope of living forever with Christ. Because we have an intimate relationship with Christ, we can enjoy these blessings now." [24]

You only have to believe and receive by faith. This is your inheritance. And you can enjoy it now!

2. Reflect and consider your position in and because of Christ. What do these truths mean to you today?

- The supremacy of Christ over all creation –

- The finished work on the cross –

- The promised gift of the Holy Spirit –

- The blessing of inheritance now –

Our hearts should burn like fire as we contemplate this incredible gift of His love for us, the blessing of our inheritance, now and forevermore.

Yes, Jacob failed. He, at times, had a weak faith and responded in the flesh. But he did not lose his position given by God. When pushed and pressed, we too sometimes cave to the natural desires, the old self and our sinful nature. This does not forfeit the love of God, nor do we lose our position in Christ. Quite the contrary.

In his book, *Gentle and Lowly*, Dane Ortlund says, "Come to me, says Christ. I will embrace you into my deepest being and never let you go." [25] Even when we sin, even when we operate out of fear and lack of faith, He wants us to come to Him. He desires to welcome us with open arms, bringing us to repentance and restoration. This is the very heart of God.

Believers can be called "the firstborn who are enrolled in Heaven," since they share the privileges of the Son (Hebrews 12:23). [26]

Remember who Jesus is. Remember who you are in Christ. Open your heart and your hands and receive every spiritual blessing He has for you. Right here, right now.

Blessed to Be a Blessing

Take a moment today to ponder the blessing of the firstborn. Reflect back on what it meant in the life of Jacob. Consider what it means for you.

Over the course of the next few days, read Ephesians 1 several times and in multiple translations. As you read, jot down the spiritual blessings you have in Christ. Encourage your child, a friend, or a relative, or someone who needs an extra dose of encouragement to do the same.

Then make verses 15 through 23 a prayer of thanksgiving and supplication for both of you. Meet for coffee or chat on the phone about what you wrote down. Commit to pray this passage of Scripture for them in the days ahead.

As children of God, we are positioned as "firstborns" by God, through Jesus. God's inheritance is fully ours!

He astounds and sustains us with His endless kindness. Only as we walk ever deeper into this tender kindness can we live the Christian life as the New Testament calls us to. Only as we drink down the kindness of the heart of Christ will we leave in our wake, everywhere we go, the aroma of Heaven, and die one day having startled the world with glimpses of a divine kindness too great to be boxed in by what we deserve. [27]
~ Dane Ortlund

JACOB IS BLESSED
Genesis 32-36

It is no surprise that the theme of blessing shapes the whole narrative of the Bible...
Like a golden thread, the power of blessing weaves the Scriptures together. [1]
~ Alan Wright

As I was writing this lesson, I found myself working backward and writing this Introduction last, after all of the other studying and writing was finished. And in the spirit of vulnerability, I think it's because I have wrestled with writing this lesson.

I'm not referring to your average, run-of-the-mill writer's block. Nor was it a wrestling of frustration with God. But there is a vastness to the story of Jacob. This "deceiver" turned patriarch is not just a character in the book of Genesis. And his aloof brother Esau is not just some antagonist in the story. What we learn about these two brothers is that their choices reverberate throughout history.

There is a fancy term among biblical scholars when referring to a method of interpreting Scripture called "Christological hermeneutic." Pete Greig put this into words I can understand: "A Christological hermeneutic means reading the Bible with your Jesus goggles on." [2]

During this study, as we have read through Genesis and combed the Scriptures seeking the full counsel of God, we have done so wearing our Jesus goggles. We seek to interpret Scripture through the lens of what Jesus has done and the redemption He has provided. Jesus is found on the pages of the Old Testament just as clearly and fully as He is found on the pages of the New Testament.

This week, as we complete our study and explore the lives of Jacob and Esau, we will see two estranged brothers whose relationship has been marred by jealousy, greed, manipulation, competition, and pride.

As their story draws to a close, we will find that there is a Redeemer Who has been at work all along, Who continues to surprise us with His goodness.

Isn't that what keeps us coming back to the Lord? When we want to walk away. When it doesn't feel worth the wrestling. When we feel we are right, and our brother is wrong. When we fear that everything we have worked for could be washed away by the ugliness of our past…

Right there, in the midst of that mess, we find that we are tethered to the One Who is true. And in Him, we find *The Blessing*.

Genesis 32

I once heard Anne Graham Lotz speak to a group of women about an experience she had with one of her grandchildren. She had taken one of the older grandchildren on a trip with her for a speaking engagement. The youngest, eager to do everything the big kids got to do, wanted to travel with her as well. Anne felt the boy was too young for a major trip, but knowing she would be taking an extensive break from travel, she told him, "You can go with me on my next trip."

A few short months later, Anne was unexpectedly asked to travel for a speaking engagement. Her grandson came to her in excitement, ready to cash in on the promise made. However, Anne told him, "I'm so sorry, but it's still too soon for you to travel. You can go on the next one." Her grandson hung his head, tears welling in his eyes, and he said, "But Grandma, YOU said I could go THIS time."[3]

Needless to say, when reminded of her promise, Anne kept her word and they had a wonderful trip together.

Read Genesis 32:1-12.

1. What does Jacob remind God of in verse 9?

2. What does Jacob remind God of again in verse 12?

God does not forget. But something happens when He sees that we have not forgotten His promises either. Our faith grows when we recall what God has spoken over us and plead with Him that He will make good on those promises.

And just like Anne's grandson, something happens in the heart of God when His child comes to Him with the words, "YOU said…"

In this conversation, Jacob is asking God to make good on His promise to him about his future. He comes to God, seemingly fully assured in God's ability to preserve him and his family just as He promised He would. But...just to "be on the safe side," Jacob devises a plan.

Read Genesis 32:13-22.

3. Summarize Jacob's backup plan below – just in case God doesn't come through.

If this isn't completely on brand for our guy, Jacob! He has been greatly humbled during his stay with Laban, but old habits die hard, and once again he is devising a plan to make sure he gets what he thinks he needs, without God's help.

We really aren't that different from Jacob, are we? We come to God, desperate for Him to move. We remind Him of His promises to us, and ask Him to let us see those promises come through the way we hope they will. We come to our Savior, hat in hand, and we plead with Him to move in ways that only He can. For Him to "open doors that no man can shut and shut doors no man can open" (Revelation 3:7). But then, how often do we come up with a plan to make things happen just in case God doesn't move on our behalf?

J. Vernon McGee writes about the struggle to trust God:

> Jacob has prayed to God and has reminded the Lord, "You told me to return to my country. You said You would protect me." But does he believe God? No. He goes right ahead and makes these arrangements, which reveals that He isn't trusting God at all. I am afraid that we are often in the same position. Many of us take our burdens to the Lord in prayer. We just spread them out before Him – I do that. Then when we get through praying, we get right up and put each little burden right back on our back and start out again with them. We don't really believe Him, do we? We don't really trust Him as we should. [4]

4. Is there a situation you're praying about now that you are tempted to try to fix on your own? Is there a prayer request you've half-heartedly given to God, not quite sure He can/will come through?

What happens next with Jacob is what always happens in this situation – we wind up wrestling with God.

Read Genesis 32:24-32.

Without a doubt, this goes down as one of the oddest moments in Scripture – and such a pivotal moment at that.

5. Combine the description of verse 24 and verse 30. Who is Jacob wrestling with?

6. What does Jacob ask of God? (v. 29)

This encounter has passed the point of wrestling. Now, Jacob is just holding on for dear life. He is finally seeing his life through the lens of God's power and God's plan. And he is unwilling to move forward without being touched by God. So he holds on. "He found out that you do not get anywhere with God by struggling and resisting. The only way that you get anywhere with Him is by yielding and just holding on to Him…When you are willing to hold on, He is there ready to help you." [5]

7. Describe a time or situation in which you found yourself wrestling with God.

8. What was the result of that wrestling?

When you find yourself wrestling with God – when you are experiencing unrest or pain in your soul where you thought God had promised to give you peace – hold on.

Up to this point, we have known Jacob as a deceiver. He has manipulated his blessing to get what he wants – and God finally breaks him. Why? So He can use him.

Watchman Nee explains the significance of brokenness in our lives:

> It is simply in the particular area where we have been disciplined by the Holy Spirit and broken by the Lord that we can touch another. If we have not been broken by the Lord in a particular thing, we can in no wise supply that need to our Christian brother….If God has put a desire in your heart to serve Him, you should understand what is involved. The way of service lies in brokenness. [6]

For Jacob, the result of his brokenness was a new name, a blessing, and a limp. For those of you who have walked with the Lord for any length of time, you've discovered the blessing of the limp. The reminder, albeit a painful one, of what God has brought you through.

At the end of our questioning, at the end of our confusion, at the end of our loneliness, uncertainty, struggling, and wrestling, we will always find the final truth – God rules.

For Jacob, this is a turning point – "God is beginning…to deal with Jacob directly in order to bring him into the place of fruit bearing and of real, vital service and witness for Him." [7]

Jacob's limp is the mark of Jesus on his life, the pre-incarnate Christ who wrestled with him, gave him a new name, and blessed him.

9. What is the new name given to Jacob? (v. 28)

There is some disagreement on the meaning of his new name, but David Guzik's commentary gives an insightful clue:

> The name Israel is a compound of two words: Sarah (meaning fight, struggle, or rule) and el (meaning, God). Some take the name Israel to mean, He who struggles with God or He who rules with God. But in Hebrew names, sometimes God is not the object of the verb but the subject. Daniel means God judges, not he judges God. This principle shows us Israel likely means, God rules. [8]

At the end of our questioning, at the end of our confusion, at the end of our loneliness, uncertainty, struggling, and wrestling, we will always find the final truth – God rules.

Genesis 33

Jacob looks up and sees Esau coming down the road toward him, along with 400 men. Imagine the tension and anxiety Jacob must feel.

1. Why might Jacob be fearful about seeing his brother after all this time?

Read Genesis 33:1-4.

2. In what order does he put each of the groups in his company?

I mean, poor Leah, right? I can't help but feel for this woman who is continually considered second-rate by Jacob. In his fear, Jacob reverts back to his plan to fix this situation himself, by arranging his family and possessions in a strategic way and preparing gifts to serve as a peace offering.

However, then Jacob seems to have a burst of courage, and maybe even is reminded of the promise of God. Because thankfully, and somewhat inexplicably, Jacob changes his approach at the last minute.

3. After arranging his family ahead of him, what does Jacob decide to do instead? (v. 3)

Have you ever heard the phrase "Do it afraid"? More than 360+ times in Scripture, God tells us – commands us – to not be afraid. But I believe that the reason we see this repeated so many times in Scripture is because God knows this will be an area where we struggle. When He places a calling on our lives, when He calls us to move, when He impresses on us the conviction to seek restoration in a broken relationship – there comes a moment when obedience must trump the emotion. We remember God's promise to be with us wherever we go, and we do it afraid. I think that's what Jacob knows he has to do here.

4. What does Jacob do when he reaches Esau?

When we allow God to break us, the fruit is always humility. Without a doubt, Jacob's wrestling match with God was the moment of breaking he needed in order to have any hope of a peaceful reunion with Esau.

Jill Briscoe captures the intensity of the moment:

> Jacob's cringing approach to his brother with slow steps interspersed with prostrations was indicative of his total sense of humiliation. He was guilty of all manner of activities against his brother and he was ready at last to admit it...He did what was right and thereby showed that the wrestling with the Lord had not been in vain. [9]

5. What is Esau's response to seeing Jacob? (v. 4)

When we allow God to break us, the fruit is always humility.

Esau has been absent from our storyline as we have followed the life of Jacob to this point. But clearly, God has done a work in his heart as well. As I read verse 4, I'm struck with the same imagery as the story of the prodigal son in Luke 15. When the son returns to his father after rebelling and wandering, he expects punishment and rejection. But instead, like Jacob, he receives the embrace of the very one he feared. Derek Kidner walks us through this reunion:

> The meeting is classic of reconciliation. The stream of gifts and the demure family procession almost comically over-organized (as it turned out) give some idea of the load on Jacob's conscience and the sure grace of Esau's reply. Guilt and forgiveness are so eloquent in every movement of the mutual approach that our Lord could find no better model for the prodigal's father at this point than Esau (Luke 15:20). [10]

Read Genesis 33:5-17.

6. How is this exchange different from what we observed between these two brothers during the whole "give me your birthright for some stew" fiasco?

Before, the relationship between these brothers was defined by take, take, take. Now, they can't seem to persuade each other to take the gifts they are offering one another. To me, there seems to be an underlying awkwardness in the whole exchange. There is a sense of relief that this decades-long feud is over, but Jacob seems to have no real desire for full restoration, at least not geographically.

7. Why might Jacob want to keep some measure of distance between him and his brother?

Have you ever been in a relationship that, for one reason or another, was broken beyond the point of restoration? While God always calls us to forgiveness, sometimes there is wisdom in not seeking full restoration. The call and blessing on Jacob's life had never included Esau. Perhaps he knows that he needs to continue his journey with God separate from Esau.

Read Genesis 33:18-20.

8. How does Jacob arrive at Shechem? (v. 18)

After all of his travels, all of his wrestling, worrying, and fear – Jacob has arrived safely in the Promised Land.

If you have a personal relationship with Christ – if you have surrendered your life to Him and received His free gift of salvation – you have arrived safely in the Promised Land. Christ in you is your "hope of glory" (Colossians 1:27). There is no safer path than following the Lord wherever He guides you, and despite the troubles along the way, there is nowhere more peaceful and secure than walking next to the Lord.

Fanny Crosby authored the hymn, "Safe in the Arms of Jesus" in which the chorus says, "Safe in the arms of Jesus, safe on His gentle breast, there by His love o'ershaded, sweetly my soul shall rest." Erin Davis writes about the greatness of Crosby's faith:

> Blind since infancy, Fanny must have faced more than her fair share of fiery trials. And yet, in addition to penning more than 5,000 hymns declaring the sufficiency of God, she is known to have uttered these faith-filled words: "Do you know that if at birth I had been able to make one petition, it would have been that I was born blind?...Because when I get to Heaven, the first face that shall ever gladden my sight will be that of my Savior." Fanny spent her life in the dark, but never alone. [11]

During all our travels, all of our wrestling, worrying, and fear – we are never alone. We are walking with our Lord in the Promised Land, and one day, we will arrive safely in His arms.

day three

Genesis 34-35:8

If I was going to title today's lesson, I think I would call it, "When God is with You Anyway." What we're about to read is one of those stories that brings assurance that the Bible is God-breathed and not man-breathed. Because if it was up to the men in this story, I feel certain this part would've been left out.

Read Genesis 34:1-30. It's a large section of Scripture, but with the drama that is about to unfold, it's quite the page-turner.

1. Summarize below why Jacob's sons commit this horrible deed.

These apples have not fallen too far from the tree. Just like a younger Jacob once did, they take matters into their own hands. But why is Jacob's family in Shechem in the first place? Warren Wiersbe comments on Jacob's delayed obedience:

> God's command was that Jacob return to Bethel (Genesis 31:13) and then to his home where Isaac still lives, which was Hebron (Genesis 35:27). Instead, he tarried first at Succoth and then settled near Shechem...It's obvious Jacob wasn't in a hurry to obey God and return to Bethel...While he tarried in that part of the land, his daughter Dinah was raped and two of his sons became murderers. It was an expensive detour. [12]

Isn't that how our flesh usually works against our desire for obedience? Satan talks us into stopping just short of what God has called us to do and to be for His glory. But anything just short of obedience is still total disobedience. And anytime we are outside of God's will for our lives, we are outside of His covering.

So why would I title this lesson, "When God is With You Anyway"? Let's move on from the carnage of this scene to see what happens next for Jacob.

Read Genesis 35:1-8.

2. What instruction does God give Jacob?

3. Before they begin this journey, what is the first word of instruction Jacob gives his family? (v. 2)

Turn to Psalm 51 and read verses 7-13.

4. What is the first thing David asks God to do after his confession in verses 7-9? (v. 10)

5. What is his commitment after he has been cleansed? (v. 13)

I think David knows what Jacob knows – redemption is drawing near. But first, a cleansing. Jacob is aware that sin has entered the camp. They have taken their eyes off of God. And they need Him to cleanse them before they can fully commit to the journey ahead.

6. What does Jacob say about the character of God in Genesis 35:3?

Tim Keller writes, "For when all is said and done on the subject of a successful Christian walk, it can be summed up in one sentence. 'Live ever aware of God's presence.'" [13] There is a principle of our faith that appears with such subtle consistency, we may have missed it in all of our Bible reading activities. It's something that undergirds the story of God from Creation to Conquest, from Wandering to Worship, from Lament to Revelation. This underlying story within the story is so central to who God is, yet it is typically overlooked in our daily lives.

What could possibly be so crucial to our foundation, yet so easily forgotten?

The awareness of God's presence in our lives. And the fact that He is with us, in spite of ourselves – when we royally mess up, when we forget our calling, when we stop short of obedience – somehow, some way, for reasons we will never understand, God is with us anyway.

Jacob realizes how true this promise has been after a crisis drives him to reflect on God's presence with him in the fire.

7. What do other nations think about Jacob's family as they journey toward Bethel? (v. 5)

Wiersbe notes, "When God's people are doing God's will God's way, they can depend on God's provision and protection. When we fear God, we need fear no one else." [14]

8. What does Jacob do upon arriving in Bethel? (v. 7)

This is a familiar place for Jacob – a place where he had once already built an altar. Returning to this place where God had met with him must have been a surreal, holy moment for Jacob. God has called him back to the place where He had assured him of His presence with him, and there is no doubt that the nostalgia of that moment would have flooded Jacob's emotions.

Several years ago, I worked at the Memphis Zoo, and there is a spot there that is so special to me because I can distinctly remember sensing God walking with me there during a particularly difficult season. One sunny day, I went for a walk, and as I could see my shadow, I just knew that the Lord was walking beside me – it was as real as if I could see His shadow next to me.

To this day, I'll occasionally feel the need to go for a walk at the zoo. Interestingly enough, because of some renovations, the road where I remember that particular walk with God is no longer there. But to me, it will always be the place I remember God's willingness to reassure me of His presence.

As Jacob looks up in his present state, despite the physical and spiritual carnage around him – murder, idolatry, revenge, jealousy – he can look back and see that God has made good on His promises. God was with him anyway.

day four

Genesis 35:22-36:43

We close this section of Genesis with the tale of two houses. The house of Jacob and the house of Esau. As we have observed throughout this study, this family is the picture of dysfunction. But what somehow still rings true, despite our shortcomings, is that God's mercy and sovereign plan never lets us go.

The House of Jacob

Read Genesis 35:22b-29.

1. In the chart below, fill in the names of Jacob's twelve sons. Then identify their mothers.

Jacob's Twelve Sons	Their Mothers

We have a tendency to romanticize the "twelve sons of Jacob" because they go on to be the "twelve tribes of Israel," and there is much in Scripture about these tribes as God's chosen people. Knowing what you know about these sons at this stage in the story, have you seen anything that would cause you to think they have earned or deserve such a high place in God's story? Of course not. That's what mercy looks like – not getting what we deserve.

Whether we say it out loud or not, we often have thoughts of what we think we deserve. "I deserve more recognition...I deserve to be paid more than this...I don't deserve what was done to me!" As I've heard my pastor's wife say many times, "We should all be glad that we don't get what we really deserve."

2. Read Genesis 12:6-7, Deuteronomy 30:5, and Joshua 11:23. Based on these verses, summarize below the promise from God and how it comes to fruition.

Hundreds of years will pass before the descendants of Abraham, Isaac, and Jacob will find their way into the Promised Land. But one thing they can be sure of as they arrive: it is God alone who has brought them there. "God will use this family, but not because they were such great or spiritual men, but because He chose them by His grace alone." [15]

3. How have you seen God move in your life in ways that the only explanation was God's hand at work?

The House of Esau

Read Genesis 36.

Raise your hand if you read the chapter in its entirety, without skimming? I know, I know. This is not the most riveting chapter in our study. But a closer look tells us an interesting story of what becomes of the house of Esau.

4. What clarification is repeated in verses 1, 8, and 43?

Anytime we see repetition like this in Scripture, it should cause us to pause. The writer seems to be taking special care to remind us that Esau is Edom. David Guzik provides some helpful background:

> The name "Edom" comes from a Semitic word meaning "red," and the land south of the Dead Sea was given that name because of the red sandstone so prominent in the topography. Esau, because of the soup for which he traded his birthright, became known as Edom, and later moved his family into the hill country of the same name. Esau became the father of the Edomites, and Jacob became the father of the Israelites, and the two nations continued to struggle through most of their history. [16]

Since the beginning, Esau was a man who followed the promptings of his flesh (Genesis 25:30-34), and as we saw in Lesson Seven, his descendants, the Edomites, followed in his footsteps.

Read Numbers 20:14-21.

5. According to this passage, what has become of the relationship between the descendants of Jacob and Esau?

Guzik writes, "Throughout all of history, we see a burning hatred of Edom against Israel. It is for this reason that Edom is frequently presented as a representation of all the nations that hated the Jews." [17]

From the moment we met Esau, he "despised his birthright" (Genesis 25:34). He has had no regard for the blessing that God could bestow on him. Jacob, while he went about it by ignoble means, was desperate for the blessing. In the end, both were blessed – one superficially, the other eternally.

6. What can we gather about how life has turned out for Esau in Genesis 36:6-8?

7. To get a sample of Esau's lineage, read Genesis 36:15-17, 21, 29-31. What types of nobility do you see?

Esau had acquired wives, wealth, possessions, and his family line was filled with powerful people. But what good is all of that when you have walked away from the blessing of God?

Ian Thomas explains the futility of Esau's achievements:

> God can do nothing with a man who will not admit that he needs anything from God… This is the basic attitude of sin – it makes God irrelevant to the stern business of living and gives to man a flattering sense of self-importance…God can do nothing for the man eaten up with the spirit of Esau. The sad thing is that even a Christian may be so impressed with himself and with his own ability that even though he gives lip service to the fact, he may still see no personal relevance in the indwelling presence of Christ. [18]

8. How can trusting our own abilities, instead of relying on Christ, lead to our downfall?

While studying about this line of nobility, I came across a familiar descendant of Esau – one that illustrates just how deep and long-lasting this enmity between the two houses ran. Briscoe shares an interesting piece of history:

> It is surely no coincidence that the age-old antagonism between Esau and Jacob should be perpetuated into the time of Christ. When Jesus stood before Herod, He was standing in the line of Jacob before a man who stood firmly in the line of Esau, for Herod was an Idumaean (the Greek equivalent of Edomite). It was left to this descendant of Esau to heap the ultimate shame on the Son of God. [19]

There is one more notable name in this line of Esau that is worth our pause.

9. Read Genesis 36:16. Who is the third chief listed?

Does this name ring a bell? Amalek is the father of a people known in other portions of Scripture as the Amalekites, and they, too, are an archnemesis of Israel.

Elsewhere in Scripture, Amalek is a man who is constantly in the way of God's people. Always standing between them and the blessing. Amalek is a picture of the flesh as Thomas writes:

> In Exodus 17, we see that no sooner had God given water to His people from the rock that Moses smote and, "then came Amalek and fought with Israel in Rephidim." Amalek here is a picture of the flesh, seeking at all costs to bar the onward journey of God's redeemed people, through the wilderness, into the land of promise…The flesh contests every attempt of the Spirit of God to lead you on into spiritual maturity. Standing across your pathway from the very outset of your Christian life is Amalek! [20]

What is your "Amalek"? What is your "Edomite"? What has the enemy of Christ placed in your path to keep you from living out your purpose? The lust of the eyes, the lust of the flesh, and the pride of life (1 John 2:16) will always attempt to stand in the way of what God is calling us to. But the enemy has already been defeated – the way of the flesh always leads to death.

Choose life.

The Blessing of Restoration

I will restore to you the years that the swarming locust has eaten, the hopper,
the destroyer, and the cutter, my great army, which I sent among you.
Joel 2:25, ESV

For the believer who wishes to bless others, there is simply no way around the wilderness of brokenness. The path to the blessing is always through the valley, and the season of stripping always comes before the sweet season of restoration. The longer you walk with Jesus, the more you begin to appreciate the brokenness, the valley, and the stripping, because you know it's all to prepare you for something greater on the other side – a closeness with God you could've never experienced otherwise.

You may have noticed we skipped a significant portion of Scripture during our homework this week – maybe even the heart of the message. Let's close our study by taking a final look at the blessing Jacob receives from the Lord.

Read Genesis 35:9-10.

1. Where has Jacob been when God appeared to him and blessed him? (v. 9)

This area is more commonly known as Upper Mesopotamia. It is no short distance from the place of Jacob's birth – the Promised Land. It is likely that during his journeys, Jacob has traveled hundreds, if not thousands, of miles before arriving home. But when his journey ends, he is welcomed by God and the blessing is reinforced.

2. Do you ever find yourself feeling distant from God?

3. When you return to God, what do you find to be true about His love for you?

Read Genesis 35:11-15.

4. Who is doing the giving here?

5. How is God able to accomplish this? (v. 11)

Wiersbe writes,

> Jacob's restoration was now complete. He was back in the place of God's choosing; he had offered himself and his sacrifices to the Lord; the Lord had spoken to him; and the covenant promises had been reaffirmed. He had come from the house of Laban to the house of God, and though he still had much to learn about his walk with the Lord, Jacob was starting to be "Israel" and live like a prince instead of a pauper. [21]

Read Genesis 35:13-22.

6. What tragedy takes place right after Jacob is blessed? (v. 19)

What Jacob realized at Peniel and here again in Bethel is that we are not "blessed" because of who we are or what our circumstances are. We are blessed because God Almighty walks with us. When we are saved, it is not by our works but by His grace (Ephesians 2:8-9) – simply because He loves us. As Hosea said, He wounds us, but He will bandage us (Hosea 6:1). When we come to the end of ourselves, that is where God is waiting to give us the blessing. Note Thomas' insight:

> Graduating from the school of despair, Jacob wrestled with a man who touched his thigh and asked him, "What is your name?" And Jacob whispered hoarsely, "Cheat – Sneak – Twister – Thief – Supplanter – that is my name!" And God said, in effect, "Jacob, that is all I have been waiting for; I have been waiting for you to call yourself by your own name – and now I will change it! You will be called Israel – Prince of God!" [22]

What does it mean to you to be "blessed"? Do you post on social media "#blessed" when things are going your way? When the prayer is answered the way you'd hoped? When you get the promotion, or your child wins the championship?

When we come to the end of ourselves, that is where God is waiting to give us the blessing.

Jacob's limp was forever a reminder of how far he had gotten from the Promised Land. He had taken the long way, and it had cost him dearly. But in that brokenness, he was blessed – truly blessed.

Blessed to Be a Blessing

When was a time that God blessed you in a way that, at the time, did not seem like a blessing? What is a limp that God allowed you to have that reminds you that He is with you? God's nearness, His presence in the heart of every believer, is the real blessing. No matter what this day looks like, you are blessed because God Almighty walks with you.

Psalm 40:10 says, "I have not hidden Your righteousness within my heart; I have spoken of Your faithfulness and Your salvation; I have not concealed Your lovingkindness and Your truth from the great congregation."

Share with someone today how you have been "blessed anyway." Even when your outward circumstances may be filled with wrestling, with mourning, with family difficulties, or with personal failure – God will come through in spite of yourself. And when He does, remember to share about His faithfulness and His salvation with "the great congregation."

How to Become a Christian

Dear one, has there ever been a time that you have given your heart to the Lord? Do you have the assurance that if you were to die right now, you would go straight to Heaven to spend all eternity in the presence of the Lord Jesus Christ and all His followers? If not, please let me share with you how you can be saved.

Admit Your Sin

First, you must understand that you are a sinner. The Bible says, "All have sinned and fall short of the glory of God" (Romans 3:23). In Romans 6:23 the Bible says, "For the wages of sin is death." That means that sin has separated us from a Holy God and we are under the sentence of eternal death and separation from God.

Abandon Self-Effort

Secondly, you must understand that you cannot save yourself by your own efforts. The Bible is very clear that it is "not by works of righteousness which we have done, but according to His mercy He saved us" (Titus 3:5, KJV). Again, in Ephesians 2:8-9 the Bible says, "For by grace you have been saved through faith; and that not of yourselves, it is the gift of God; not as a result of works, so that no one may boast."

Acknowledge Christ's Payment

Thirdly, you must believe that Jesus Christ, the Son of God, died for your sins. The Bible says, "God demonstrates His own love toward us, in that while we were yet sinners, Christ died for us" (Romans 5:8). That means He died a sacrificial death in your place. Your sin debt has been paid by the blood of Jesus Christ, which "cleanses us from all sin" (1 John 1:7).

Accept Him as Savior

Fourthly, you must put your faith in Jesus Christ and Him alone for your salvation. The blood of Christ does you no good until you receive Him by faith. The Bible says, "Believe in the Lord Jesus, and you will be saved" (Acts 16:31).

Has there been a time in your life that you have taken this all-important step of faith? If not, I urge you to do it right now. Jesus Christ is the only way to Heaven. He said, "I am the way, the truth, and the life. No one can come to the Father except through Me" (John 14:6, NLT).

Would you like to become a Christian? Would you like to invite Jesus Christ to come into your heart today? Read over this prayer and if it expresses the desire of your heart, you may ask Him into your heart to take away your sin, fill you with His Spirit, and take you to home to Heaven when you die. If this is your intention, pray this prayer.

Oh God, I'm a sinner. I am lost and I need to be saved. I know I cannot save myself, so right now, once and for all, I trust You to save me. Come into my heart, forgive my sin, and make me Your child. I give You my life. I will live for You as You give me Your strength. Amen.

If you will make this your heartfelt prayer, God will hear and save you! Jesus has promised that He will never leave nor forsake anyone who comes to Him in faith. In John 6:37 He said, "The one who comes to Me I will certainly not cast out."

Welcome to the family!

End Notes

Introduction

1. Hughes, R.K. (2004). *Genesis*, p. 605. Wheaton, IL: Crossway.

2. Information regarding Michelangelo's The David retrieved from https://www.accademia.org/explore-museum/artworks/michelangelos-david/ and https://www.britannica.com/topic/David-sculpture

3. Wiersbe, W. (2010). *Be Authentic,* p. 13. Colorado Springs, CO: David C. Cook.

4. Hughes, R.K. (2004). *Genesis*, p. 15. Wheaton, IL: Crossway.

5. Wiersbe, W. (1997). *Be Basic,* p. 12. Colorado Springs, CO: David C. Cook Publishing.

6. Skinner, R.D. (2018). *Studies in Genesis,* p. 44. (Michael Spradlin, Ed.). Collierville, TN: Innovo Publishing.

7. Swindoll, C. (n.d.). "Genesis," *Insight for Living Ministries.* Retrieved from https://insight.org/resources/bible/the-pentateuch/genesis

8. Champlin, M. (n.d.). "A Biblical Theology of Blessing in Genesis," *The Gospel Coalition.* Retrieved from https://www.thegospelcoalition.org/themelios/article/a-biblical-theology-of-blessing-in-genesis/

9. Wiersbe, W. (2008). *Bless You*, p. 8. Grand Rapids, MI: Discovery House Publishers.

10. Hamilton, V. (1982). *Handbook on the Pentateuch*, p. 18. Grand Rapids, MI: Baker.

11. McKeown, J. (2008). *Genesis*, p. 222. Grand Rapids, Eerdmans.

12. Hughes, R.K. (2004). *Genesis*, p. 605. Wheaton, IL: Crossway.

Lesson 1

1. Batterson. M. (2013). *All in*, p. 13-14. Grand Rapids, MI: Zondervan.

2. Carmichael, A. (2013). "Make Me Thy Fuel" (poem), *Toward Jerusalem*, Loc 1480. (Kindle) Fort Washington, PA: CLC Publishing.

3. Hughes, K. (2004). *Genesis*, p. 181-182. Wheaton, IL: Crossway.

4. Swindoll, C. (2014). *Abraham*, p. 2. Carol Stream, IL: Tyndale House Publishers, Inc.

5. Phillips, J. (1980). *Exploring Genesis*, p. 106. Chicago, IL: Moody Press.

6. Meyer, F.B. (1996). *The Life of Abraham*, p. 12. Lynnwood, WA: Emerald Books.

7. Lawler, A. (March 11, 2016). "City of Biblical Abraham Brimmed with Trade and Riches," *National Geographic*. Retrieved from https://www.nationalgeographic.com/adventure article/160311-ur-iraq-trade-royal-cemetery-woolley-archaeology

8. *New World Encyclopedia*. (n.d.) Retrieved from https://www.newworldencyclopedia.org/ entry/sin-(mythology)

9. Gibson, J.L. (1999). *God's Word for the Biblically-Inept: Genesis*, p. 106. Lancaster, PA: Starburst Publishers.

10. Kidner, D. (1967). *Genesis, An Introduction and Commentary*, p. 113. London, England: The Tyndale Press.

11. Meyer, F.B. (1996). *The Life of Abraham*, p. 25. Lynnwood, WA: Emerald Books.

12. Swindoll, C. (2014). *Abraham*, p. 13. Carol Stream, IL: Tyndale House Publishers, Inc.

13. Swindoll, C. (2014). *Abraham*, p. 11. Carol Stream, IL: Tyndale House Publishers, Inc.

14. Hendricks, H. (1972). *The Battle of the Gods,* p. 41. Chicago: IL: Moody Press.

15. Meyer, F.B. (1996). *The Life of Abraham*, p. 28. Lynnwood, WA: Emerald Books.

16. Hughes, K. (2004). *Genesis*, p. 185. Wheaton, IL: Crossway.

17. Hughes, K. (2004). *Genesis*, p. 186. Wheaton, IL: Crossway.

18. Wiersbe, W. (1991). *Be Obedient*, p. 26. Colorado Springs, CO: David C. Cook.

19. Shechem in the O.T. is believed by most scholars to be have been about a mile west of Jacob's well and Sychar was about a half a mile north of the well.

20. Hughes, K. (2004). *Genesis*, p. 186. Wheaton, IL: Crossway.

21. Elwell, W. (ed.) (1988). *Baker Encyclopedia* of the Bible, p. 11. Grand Rapids, MI: Baker Books.

22. Hughes, K. (2004). *Genesis*, p. 187. Wheaton, IL: Crossway.

23. Reynolds, W.J. (1991). *The Baptist Hymnal*, p. 305. Convention Press: Nashville, TN. (Liberties taken).

24. Swindoll, C. (2014). *Abraham*, p. 18. Carol Stream, IL: Tyndale House Publishers, Inc.

25. Swindoll, C. (2014). *Abraham*, p. 18. Carol Stream, IL: Tyndale House Publishers, Inc.

26. Meyer, F.B. (1996). *The Life of Abraham*, p. 41-42. Lynnwood, WA: Emerald Books.

27. Hughes, K. (2004). *Genesis*, p. 190. Wheaton, IL: Crossway.Swindoll, C. (2014). *Abraham*, p. 21. Carol Stream, IL: Tyndale House Publishers, Inc.

28. Phillips, J. (1980). *Exploring Genesis*, p. 119. Chicago, IL: Moody Press.

29. Carmichael, A. (2009). *Edges of His Ways*, p. 30. Fort Washington, PA: CLC Publishing.

30. Warner, M. & Wilder, J. (2016). *Rare Leadership*. Chicago, IL: Moody Press. See Chapter 7, "Remain Relational" for a further discussion on the subject.

31. Hughes, K. (2004). *Genesis*, p. 200. Wheaton, IL: Crossway.

32. Warner, M. & Wilder, J. (2016). *Rare Leadership*, p. 136. Chicago, IL: Moody Press.

33. Warner, M. & Wilder, J. (2016). *Rare Leadership*. Chicago, IL: Moody Press. See Chapter 7, "Remain Relational" for a further discussion on the subject.

34. Hughes, K. (2004). *Genesis*, p. 201. Wheaton, IL: Crossway.

35. Wiersbe, W. (1991). *Be Obedient*, p. 39. Colorado Springs, CO: David C. Cook.

36. Elliot, E. (n.d.). *Good Reads*. Retrieved from https://www.goodreads.com/author/quotes/6264. Elisabeth_Elliot

37. Wiersbe, W. (1991). *Be Obedient*, p. 9. Colorado Springs, CO: David C. Cook.

38. Wiersbe, W. (1991). *Be Obedient*, p. 9-10. Colorado Springs, CO: David C. Cook.

39. Smalley, G. & Trent, J. (1987). *The Blessing*, p. 16. Nashville, TN: Thomas Nelson.

40. Gunter, S. (2017). *Blessings for Life*, p. 8. Birmingham, AL: The Father's Business.

41. Wright, A. (2021). *The Power to Bless: How to Speak Life and Empower the People You Love*, p. 16-17. Grand Rapids, MI: Baker Books.

42. Willard, D. (2014). *Living in Christ's Presence: Final Words on Heaven and the Kingdom of God*, pp. 163-169. Downer's Grove, IL: InterVarsity Press.

Lesson 2

1. Sproul, R.C. (2016). *Knowing Scripture*, p. 35. Downers Grove, IL: InterVaristy Press.

2. Meyer, F.B. (1996). *The Life of Abraham*, p. 62. Lynwood, WA: Emerald Books

3. Spence, H.D.M. and J. Exell. (2004). *The Pulpit Commentary, Vol. 1: Genesis, Exodus*, Logos. Peabody, MA: Hendrickson.

4. Wiersbe, W.W. (1991) *Be Obedient, Learning the Secret of Living by Faith*, p. 45. Colorado Springs, CO: David C. Cook.

5. Wiersbe, W.W. (1991) *Be Obedient, Learning the Secret of Living by Faith*, p. 49. Colorado Springs, CO: David C. Cook.

6. Spence, H.D.M. and J. Exell. (2004). *The Pulpit Commentary, Vol. 1: Genesis, Exodus*, Logos. Peabody, MA: Hendrickson.

7. Lemmel, H. (1991). *The Baptist Hymnal*, p. 320. Nashville, TN: Convention Press.

8. Piper, J. (June 21, 2018). "This Day in History the Death of Hudson Taylor." *Crossway*. Retrieved from https://www.crossway.org/articles/this-day-in-history-the-death-of-hudson-taylor/

9. Wiersbe, W.W. (1991) *Be Obedient, Learning the Secret of Living by Faith*, p. 61. Colorado Springs, CO: David C. Cook.

10. Hughes, R.K. (2004). *Genesis*, p. 229. (Kindle Edition). Wheaton, IL: Crossway.

11. Swindoll, C.R. (2014). *Abraham: One Nomad's Amazing Journey of Faith*, Carol Stream, IL: Tyndale House Publishers.

12. Keller, T. (Nov. 3, 1996). *Daring to Draw Near*, Gospel in Life, Retrieved from https://gospelinlife.com/downloads/abraham-and-the-torch-5860/

13. Duguid, I. (1999). *Living in the Gap Between Promise and Reality*, p. 59. Phillipsburg, NJ: P & R Publishing

14. Keller, T. (May 27, 2022). *The Living Water*, Gospel in Life, Retrieved from https://www.oneplace.com/ministries/gospel-in-life/listen/the-living-water-967567.html

15. Cates, B. (1967). "Do You Really Care?", *Hymnary.org*. Retrieved from https://hymnary.org/text/i_look_around_in_the_place_where_i_live

Lesson 3
1. Gayle, C. (2021). *New Name Written Down in Glory*. Album: Endless Praise.

2. Tripp, P. (2014). *New Morning Mercies: A Daily Gospel Devotional*. ("already" and "not yet" reference found in multiple locations in the book). Wheaton, IL: Crossway Publishing.

3. Cobble, T. (2020). *The Bible Recap Podcast* by D-Group. Episode 17.

4. Anders, M. (2002). *Holman Old Testament Commentary: Genesis*, p. 148. Nashville, TN: B&H Publishing Group.

5. Guzik, D. (2008). *Genesis Commentary*. Goleta, CA: Enduring Word Media. Retrieved from enduringword.com

6. Anders, M. (2002). *Holman Old Testament Commentary: Genesis*, p. 149. Nashville, TN: B&H Publishing Group.

7. MacArthur, J. (2020). *John MacArthur Study Bible, New American Standard, Second Edition*, p. 22. Thomas Nelson. Lahabra, CA: The Lockman Foundation.

8. Harris, A. (2021). *Hagar, the Single Mom*. Retrieved from thegospelcoalition.org/article/hagar-single-mom. Posted February 3, 2021.

9. Harris, A. (2021). *Hagar, the Single Mom*. Retrieved from thegospelcoalition.org/article/hagar-single-mom. Posted February 3, 2021.

10. Wright, A. (2021). *The Power to Bless: How to Speak Life and Empower the People You Love*, p. 99. Grand Rapids, MI: Baker Publishing Group.

11. Van Loon, M. (2018). *Born to Wander: Recovering the Value of Our Pilgrim Identity*, p. 40. Chicago, IL: Moody Publishers.

12. Anders, M. (2002). *Holman Old Testament Commentary: Genesis*, p. 151. Nashville, TN: B&H Publishing Group.

13. Anders, M. (2002). *Holman Old Testament Commentary: Genesis*, p. 152. Nashville, TN: B&H Publishing Group.

14. Guzik, D. (2008). *Genesis Commentary*. Goleta, CA: Enduring Word Media. Retrieved from enduringword.com

15. Anders, M. (2002). *Holman Old Testament Commentary: Genesis*, p. 153. Nashville, TN: B&H Publishing Group.

16. Wiersbe, W. (2010). *Be Obedient: Learning the Secret of Living by Faith, Old Testament Commentary, Genesis 12–25,* p. 96. Colorado Springs, CO: David C. Cook.

17. Meyer, F.B. (1996). *The Life of Abraham*, p. 121. Lynwood, WA: Emerald Books.

18. MacArthur, J. (2020). *John MacArthur Study Bible, New American Standard, Second Edition*, p. 25. Thomas Nelson. Lahabra, CA: The Lockman Foundation.

19. Anders, M. (2002). *Holman Old Testament Commentary: Genesis*, p. 165. Nashville, TN: B&H Publishing Group.

20. MacArthur, J. (2020). *John MacArthur Study Bible, New American Standard, Second Edition*, p. 25. Thomas Nelson. Lahabra, CA: The Lockman Foundation.

21. Quoted by Steve Gaines. Bellevue Baptist Church, Bellevue.org.

22. Wiersbe, W. (2010). *Be Obedient: Learning the Secret of Living by Faith, Old Testament Commentary, Genesis 12–25,* p. 97. Colorado Springs, CO: David C. Cook.

23. Hart, B. & Risley, T. (2003). Retrieved from: https://www.aft.org/sites/ default/files/periodicals/TheEarlyCatastrophe.pdf

Lesson 4

1. Wiersbe, W. (1991). *Be Obedient: Learning the Secret of Living by Faith,* p. 101. Colorado Springs, CO: David C. Cook.

2. Fritzemeier, M. (June 13, 2017). *"Yada": Cultivating Intimacy with God.* https://www.curtlandry.com/yada-cultivating-intimacy-with-god/.

3. Voskamp, A. (2022). *Waymaker*, p. 76. Nashville, TN: W Publishing Group.

4. Phillips, J. (1980). *Exploring Genesis*, p. 159. Chicago, IL: Moody Press.

5. Wiersbe, W. (1991). *Be Obedient: Learning the Secret of Living by Faith,* p. 100. Colorado Springs, CO: David C. Cook.

6. Evans, T. (2019). *The Tony Evans Bible Commentary*, p. 74. Nashville, TN: Holman Bible Publishers.

7. Evans, T. (2019). *The Tony Evans Bible Commentary*, p. 74. Nashville, TN: Holman Bible Publishers.

8. May, I. (2014). *Daily Devotional Companion to the One Year® Chronological Bible*, p. 18. Olive Branch, MS: Chronological Bible Teaching Ministries, Inc.

9. *Life Application Study Bible, New Living Translation,* p. 48. (2007). Carol Stream, IL: Tyndale House Publishers, Inc.

10. *Life Application Study Bible, New Living Translation,* p. 48. (2007). Carol Stream, IL: Tyndale House Publishers, Inc.

11. Batterson, M. (2019). *Double Blessing*, p. 72. Colorado Springs, CO: Multnomah.

12. Batterson, M. (2019). *Double Blessing*, p. 2. Colorado Springs, CO: Multnomah.

13. Wiersbe, W. (1991). *Be Obedient: Learning the Secret of Living by Faith*, p. 109. Colorado Springs, CO: David C. Cook.

14. McGee, J. (1981). *Thru the Bible with J. Vernon McGee Vol. I,* p.85. Nashville, TN: Thomas Nelson Publishers.

15. Deffinbaugh, B. (May 12, 2004). *Don't Ever Say Never.* Retrieved from https://bible.org/seriespage/21-don-t-ever-say-never-genesis-201-18.

16. Wiersbe, W. (1991). *Be Obedient: Learning the Secret of Living by Faith,* p. 109. Colorado Springs, CO: David C. Cook.

17. Wiersbe, W. (1991). *Be Obedient: Learning the Secret of Living by Faith,* p. 110. Colorado Springs, CO: David C. Cook.

18. Wiersbe, W. (1991). *Be Obedient: Learning the Secret of Living by Faith,* p. 113. Colorado Springs, CO: David C. Cook.

19. Batterson, M. (2019). *Double Blessing*, p. 24. Colorado Springs, CO: Multnomah.

20. Batterson, M. (2019). *Double Blessing*, p. 24. Colorado Springs, CO: Multnomah.

21. Voskamp, A. (2022). *Waymaker*, p. 31. Nashville, TN: W Publishing Group.

22. Smith, M. (n.d). *Lyrics.com*. Retrieved from https://www.lyrics.com/lyric/36189713/Michael+W.+Smith/Waymaker

23. Wiersbe, W. (1991). *Be Obedient: Learning the Secret of Living by Faith,* p. 116. Colorado Springs, CO: David C. Cook.

24. Batterson, M. (2019). *Double Blessing*, p. 116. Colorado Springs, CO: Multnomah.

Lesson 5

1. Retrieved from https://www.markbatterson.com/kiss-the-wave/

2. Can be translated happy. Retrieved from https://www.blueletterbible.org/lexicon/g3107/kjv/tr/0-1/

3. Swindoll, C.R. (2014). *Abraham: One Nomad's Amazing Journey of Faith*, p. 199. Carol Stream, IL: Tyndale House Publishers.

4. Swindoll, C.R. (2014). *Abraham: One Nomad's Amazing Journey of Faith*, p. 199. Carol Stream, IL: Tyndale House Publishers.

5. Wiersbe, W. W. (1993*). Wiersbe's Expository Outlines on the Old Testament*, p. 53. Wheaton, IL: Victor Books.

6. Phillips, J. (2009). *Exploring Genesis: An Expository Commentary,* p. 182. Grand Rapids, MI: Kregel Publications.

7. Phillips, J. (2009). *Exploring Genesis: An Expository Commentary,* p. 182. Grand Rapids, MI: Kregel Publications.

8. Phillips, J. (2009). *Exploring Genesis: An Expository Commentary,* p. 179. Grand Rapids, MI: Kregel Publications.

9. Rogers, A. (2017). *An Old Testament Calvary.* In *Adrian Rogers Sermon Archive* (Genesis 22:1–2). Signal Hill, CA: Rogers Family Trust.)

10. Wiersbe, W. (1960). *Be Obedient*, p. 138. Colorado Springs, CO: David C. Cook.

11. Wiersbe, W. (1960). *Be Obedient*, p. 137. Colorado Springs, CO: David C. Cook.

12. Phillips, J. (2009). *Exploring Genesis: An Expository Commentary,* p 184. Grand Rapids, MI: Kregel Publications.

13. Rogers, A. (2017)."Till Death Do Us Part." In *Adrian Rogers Sermon Archive* (Genesis 23:1-2). Signal Hill, CA: Rogers Family Trust.

14. Meyer, F.B. (1996). *The Life of Abraham*, p. 173. Lynwood, WA: Emerald Books.

15. Wiersbe, W. (1960). *Be Obedient*, p. 156. Colorado Springs, CO: David C. Cook.

16. Wiersbe, W. (1960). *Be Obedient*, p. 156. Colorado Springs, CO: David C. Cook.

17. Wiersbe, W. (1960). *Be Obedient*, p. 156. Colorado Springs, CO: David C. Cook.

Lesson 6

1. Luther, M. (n.d.). *Christian Quotes*. Retrieved from https://www.christianquotes.info/top-quotes/18-great-christian-quotes-about-marriage/

2. Swindoll, C.R. (2014). *Abraham: One Nomad's Amazing Journey of Faith*, p 224. Carol Stream, IL: Tyndale House Publishers.

3. Phillips, J. (2009). *Exploring Genesis: An Expository Commentary,* p 190. Grand Rapids, MI: Kregel Publications.

4. Swindoll, C.R. (2014). *Abraham: One Nomad's Amazing Journey of Faith*, p 225. Carol Stream, IL: Tyndale House Publishers.

5. Wiersbe, W.W. (1991). *Be Obedient*, p 46. Wheaton, IL: Victor Books.

6. Hughes, R.K. (2004). *Genesis*, p. 318. (Kindle Edition). Wheaton, IL: Crossway.

7. Duffinbaugh, B. (n.d.). *"How to Find a Godly Wife"*. Retrieved from https://bible.org/seriespage/25-how-find-godly-wife-genesis-241-67.

8. Hughes, R.K. (2004). *Genesis*, p. 317-318. (Kindle Edition). Wheaton, IL: Crossway.

9. Duffinbaugh, B. (n.d.). *"How to Find a Godly Wife"*. Retrieved from https://bible.org/seriespage/25-how-find-godly-wife-genesis-241-67

10. Duffinbaugh, B. (n.d.). *"How to Find a Godly Wife"*. Retrieved from https://bible.org/seriespage/25-how-find-godly-wife-genesis-241-67

11. Hughes, R.K. (2004). *Genesis*, p. 320. (Kindle Edition). Wheaton, IL: Crossway.

12. Swindoll, C.R. (2014). *Abraham: One Nomad's Amazing Journey of Faith,* p 233. Carol Stream, IL: Tyndale House Publishers.

13. Swindoll, C.R. (2014). *Abraham: One Nomad's Amazing Journey of Faith*, p 234. Carol Stream, IL: Tyndale House Publishers.

14. Rogers, A. (2017). "A Bride for Isaac." In *Adrian Rogers Sermon Archive* (Ge 24). Signal Hill, CA: Rogers Family Trust.

15. Rogers, A. (2017). "A Bride for Isaac." In *Adrian Rogers Sermon Archive* (Ge 24). Signal Hill, CA: Rogers Family Trust.

16. Rogers, A. (2017). "A Bride for Isaac." In *Adrian Rogers Sermon Archive* (Ge 24). Signal Hill, CA: Rogers Family Trust.

17. Phillips, J. (2009). *Exploring Genesis: An Expository Commentary,* p.196. Grand Rapids, MI: Kregel Publications.

18. Swindoll, C.R. (2014). *Abraham: One Nomad's Amazing Journey of Faith*, p 238. Carol Stream, IL: Tyndale House Publishers.

19. Swindoll, C.R. (2014). *Abraham: One Nomad's Amazing Journey of Faith*, p 199. Carol Stream, IL: Tyndale House Publishers.

20. Swindoll, C.R. (2014). *Abraham: One Nomad's Amazing Journey of Faith*, p 240-241. Carol Stream, IL: Tyndale House Publishers.

21. Deffinbaugh, B. (n.d). "Principle of Divine Election". *Bible.org*. Retrieved from https://bible.org/seriespage/26-principle-divine-election-genesis-251-34.

22. Phillips, J. (2009). *Exploring Genesis: An Expository Commentary*, p 201-202. Grand Rapids, MI: Kregel Publications.

23. Wiersbe, W.W. (1993). *Wiersbe's Expository Outlines on the Old Testament, p 58.* Wheaton, IL: Victor Books.

24. *Virginia + Kd.com*. (n.d.). Retrieved from https://www.virginiatkd.com/a-smooth-sea-never-made-a-skilled-sailor/.

Lesson 7

1. Hughes, R.K. (2004). *Genesis*, p. 331. (Kindle Edition). Wheaton, IL: Crossway.

2. Wiersbe, W. (1997). *Be Authentic: Exhibiting Real Faith in the Real World,* p. 17-18. Colorado Springs, CO: David C. Cook.

3. Wiersbe, W. (1997). *Be Authentic: Exhibiting Real Faith in the Real World,* p. 17. Colorado Springs, CO: David C. Cook.

4. Wiersbe, W. (1997). *Be Authentic: Exhibiting Real Faith in the Real World,* p. 19. Colorado Springs, CO: David C. Cook.

5. Hughes, R.K. (2004). *Genesis*, p. 331. Wheaton, IL: Crossway.

6. Hughes, R.K. (2004). *Genesis*, p. 332. (Kindle Edition). Wheaton, IL: Crossway.

7. Kidner, D. (1967). *Genesis*, p. 151. Downers Grove, IL: Inter-Varsity Press.

8. *Shepherd's Notes: Genesis,* (1997). p. 64. Nashville, TN: B & H Publishing.

9. Wiersbe, W. (1997). *Be Authentic: Exhibiting Real Faith in the Real World,* p. 22. Colorado Springs, CO: David C. Cook.

10. Wright, A. (2021). *The Power to Bless*, p. 32. Grand Rapids, MI: Baker Books.

11. Henry, M. (n.d.) Matthew Henry Complete Commentary. *Bible Study Tools*. Retrieved from https://www.biblestudytools.com/commentaries/matthew-henry-complete/genesis/25.html

12. Phillips, J. (2009). *Exploring Genesis: An Expository Commentary,* p 214. Grand Rapids, MI: Kregel Publications.

13. Wiersbe, W. (1997). *Be Authentic: Exhibiting Real Faith in the Real World,* p. 22. Colorado Springs, CO: David C. Cook.

14. Cowper, W. (1976). "There is a Fountain Filled with Blood", *Hymns for the Family of God,* p. 263. Nashville, TN: Paragon Associates, Inc.

15. Wiersbe, W. (1997). *Be Authentic: Exhibiting Real Faith in the Real World,* p. 23. Colorado Springs, CO: David C. Cook.

16. Wiersbe, W. (1997). *Be Authentic: Exhibiting Real Faith in the Real World,* p. 23. Colorado Springs, CO: David C. Cook.

17. Phillips, J. (2009). *Exploring Genesis: An Expository Commentary,* p. 217. Grand Rapids, MI: Kregel Publications.

18. Phillips, J. (2009). *Exploring Genesis: An Expository Commentary,* p. 217. Grand Rapids, MI: Kregel Publications.

19. Wiersbe, W. (1997). *Be Authentic: Exhibiting Real Faith in the Real World,* p. 25. Colorado Springs, CO: David C. Cook.

20. Hughes, R.K. (2004). *Genesis,* p. 344. Wheaton, IL: Crossway.

21. Wiersbe, W. (1997). *Be Authentic: Exhibiting Real Faith in the Real World,* p. 28. Colorado Springs, CO: David C. Cook.

22. Dysfunctional. *Merriam-Webster.com.* Retrieved from https://www.merriam-webster.com/dictionary/dysfunctional

23. Phillips, J. (2009). *Exploring Genesis: An Expository Commentary,* p. 225. Grand Rapids, MI: Kregel Publications.

24. Phillips, J. (2009). *Exploring Genesis: An Expository Commentary,* p. 225. Grand Rapids, MI: Kregel Publications.

25. Scott, W. (2014). "Marmion." *Gutenberg,* (H. Morley, Ed.) Retrieved from https://www.gutenberg.org/files/4010/4010-h/4010-h.htm

26. Phillips, J. (2009). *Exploring Genesis: An Expository Commentary,* p. 228. Grand Rapids, MI: Kregel Publications.

27. Phillips, J. (2009). *Exploring Genesis: An Expository Commentary,* p. 228. Grand Rapids, MI: Kregel Publications.

28. Hughes, R.K. (2004). *Genesis,* p. 349. (Kindle Edition). Wheaton, IL: Crossway.

29. Phillips, J. (2009). *Exploring Genesis: An Expository Commentary,* p. 228. Grand Rapids, MI: Kregel Publications.

30. Pink, A.W. (n.d.). The Sovereignty of God, Retrieved from https://www.goodreads.com/quotes/956255-nothing-in-all-the-vast-universe-can-come-to-pass

31. This quote is generally attributed to C.S. Lewis.

32. Barnhouse, D.G. (1973). *Genesis*, p. 71. Grand Rapids, MI: Zondervan.

33. Wiersbe, W. (1997). *Be Authentic: Exhibiting Real Faith in the Real World,* p. 39. Colorado Springs, CO: David C. Cook.

34. Wiersbe, W. (1997). *Be Authentic: Exhibiting Real Faith in the Real World,* p. 39. Colorado Springs, CO: David C. Cook.

35. Phillips, J. (2009). *Exploring Genesis: An Expository Commentary,* p. 234. Grand Rapids, MI: Kregel Publications.

36. Deffinbaugh, B. (n.d.) *"The Seeker is Sought"* (Genesis 28:1-22). *Bible.org.* Retrieved from https://bible.org/seriespage/29-seeker-sought-genesis-281-22

37. Phillips, J. (2009). *Exploring Genesis: An Expository Commentary,* p. 235. Grand Rapids, MI: Kregel Publications.

38. Hughes, R.K. (2004). *Genesis*, p. 354. (Kindle Edition). Wheaton, IL: Crossway.

39. Wiersbe, W.W. (2008). *Bless you*, p. 14. Grand Rapids, MI: Discovery House Publishers.

40. Mathis, D. (January 10, 2021). "The Lord Bless You and Keep You." *Desiring God.* Retrieved from https://www.desiringgod.org/articles/the-lord-bless-you-and-keep-you

41. Wilder, J., Hendricks, M. (2020). *The Other Half of Church*, p. 54. Chicago, IL: Moody Publishers.

42. Edwards, J. (July 8, 1741). "Sinners in the Hands of an Angry God." *Blue Letter Bible.* Retrieved from: https://www.blueletterbible.org/Comm/edwards_jonathan/Sermons /Sinners.cfm

43. Wright, A. (2021). *The Power to Bless*, p. 31. Grand Rapids, MI: Baker Books.

44. Wright, A. (2021). *The Power to Bless*, p. 31. Grand Rapids, MI: Baker Books.

45. Wright, A. (2021). *The Power to Bless*, p. 19. Grand Rapids, MI: Baker Books.

46. Wright, A. (2021). *The Power to Bless*, p. 23. Grand Rapids, MI: Baker Books.

Lesson 8

1. Wiersbe, W. (1997). *Be Authentic: Exhibiting Real Faith in the Real World,* p. 47. Colorado Springs, CO: David C. Cook.

2. Wiersbe, W. (1997). *Be Authentic: Exhibiting Real Faith in the Real World,* p. 47. Colorado Springs, CO: David C. Cook.

3. Wiersbe, W. (1997). *Be Authentic: Exhibiting Real Faith in the Real World,* p. 203-204. Colorado Springs, CO: David C. Cook. [Warren Wiersbe notes that the name, Bethel, "is used in Genesis 12:8 and 13:3 because by the time Moses wrote Genesis, Bethel was the name his readers knew best."]

4. Evans, T. (2019). *The Tony Evans Bible Commentary*, p. 82. Nashville, TN: Holman Bible Publishers.

5. Wiersbe, W. (1997). *Be Authentic: Exhibiting Real Faith in the Real World,* p. 42. Colorado Springs, CO: David C. Cook.

6. Wiersbe, W. (1997). *Be Authentic: Exhibiting Real Faith in the Real World,* p. 48. Colorado Springs, CO: David C. Cook.

7. *Life Application Study Bible, New Living Translation,* p. 73. (2007). Carol Stream, IL: Tyndale House Publishers, Inc.

8. Wiersbe, W. (1997). *Be Authentic: Exhibiting Real Faith in the Real World,* p. 50. Colorado Springs, CO: David C. Cook.

9. Evans, T. (2019). *The Tony Evans Bible Commentary*, p. 84. Nashville, TN: Holman Bible Publishers.

10. Deffinbaugh, B. (May 12, 2004). "I Led Two Wives." *Bible.org.* Retrieved from https://bible.org/seriespage/30-i-led-two-wives-genesis-291-30

11. *Life Application Study Bible, New Living Translation,* p. 75. (2007). Carol Stream, IL: Tyndale House Publishers, Inc.

12. Wiersbe, W. (1997). *Be Authentic: Exhibiting Real Faith in the Real World,* p. 53. Colorado Springs, CO: David C. Cook.

13. *Life Application Study Bible, New Living Translation,* p. 74. (2007). Carol Stream, IL: Tyndale House Publishers, Inc.

14. Miller, D. (May 31, 2012). "Genesis 29, 30, 31." *Bible.org.* Retrieved from https://bible.org/seriespage/lesson-3-genesis-29-30-31.

15. Lacey, T. (April 26, 2019). Retrieved from Answersingenesis.org/Jacob's Odd "Breeding Program" of Genesis.

16. Wiersbe, W. (1997). *Be Authentic: Exhibiting Real Faith in the Real World,* p. 59. Colorado Springs, CO: David C. Cook.

17. Wiersbe, W. (1997). *Be Authentic: Exhibiting Real Faith in the Real World,* p. 56. Colorado Springs, CO: David C. Cook.

18. Wiersbe, W. (1997). *Be Authentic: Exhibiting Real Faith in the Real World,* p. 56-57. Colorado Springs, CO: David C. Cook.

19. Wiersbe, W. (1997). *Be Authentic: Exhibiting Real Faith in the Real World,* p. 56-57. Colorado Springs, CO: David C. Cook.

20. Brown, G. (April 23, 2019). *Faithfully Following God.* https://bible.org/seriespage/8-faithfully-following-god-genesis-31.

21. Lynch, J., McNicol, B., Thrall, B. (2011). "The Cure", *True Face.* p. 10. www.trueface.org.

22. Evans, T. (2019). *The Tony Evans Bible Commentary*, p. 1206. Nashville, TN: Holman Bible Publishers.

23. Evans, T. (2019). *The Tony Evans Bible Commentary*, p. 1206. Nashville, TN: Holman Bible Publishers.

24. *Life Application Study Bible, New Living Translation,* p. 2612. (2007). Carol Stream, IL: Tyndale House Publishers, Inc.

25. Ortlund, D. (2020). *Gentle and Lowly: The Heart of Christ for Sinners and Sufferers*, p. 66. Wheaton, IL: Crossway.

26. Bible.org. (n.d.). Retrieved from https://bible.org/question/what-significance-%E2%80%9C firstborn%E2%80%9D-bible

27. Ortlund, D. (2020). *Gentle and Lowly: The Heart of Christ for Sinners and Sufferers*, p. 22. Wheaton, IL: Crossway.

Lesson 9

1. Wright. A (2021) *The Power to Bless: How to Speak Life and Empower the People You Love,* p. 21. Grand Rapids, MI: Baker Books.

2. Greig, P. (2022) *That Sounds Fun Podcast: TSF Prayer Series: Pastor Pete Greig + Hearing God.*

3. Graham-Lotz, A. Story told while speaking at the 2016 Women's Session of the Southern Baptist Convention.

4. McGee, J. (1991) *Thru the Bible Commentary Series: Genesis 34-50,* p. 177. Nashville, TN: Thomas Nelson.

5. McGee, J. (1991) *Thru the Bible Commentary Series: Genesis 34-50,* p. 180. Nashville, TN: Thomas Nelson.

6. Nee, W. (2000) *The Release of the Spirit*, p. 54. New York: Christian Fellowship Publishers, Inc.

7. McGee, J. (1991) *Thru the Bible Commentary series: Genesis 34-50,* p. 173-174. Nashville, TN: Thomas Nelson.

8. Guzik, D. (2008) *Genesis Commentary*. Goleta, CA: Enduring Word Media. Retrieved from enduringword.com

9. Briscoe, J. (1987) *The Communicator's Commentary: Genesis*, p. 280-281. Waco, TX: World Books.

10. Kidner, D. (1967) *Genesis*, p. 171. Downers Grove, IL: InterVarsity Press.

11. Davis, E. (2020) "Safe in the Arms of Jesus." *She Reads Truth*. Retrieved from shereadstruth. com/safe-in-the-arms-of-jesus/.

12. Wiersbe, W. (1983) *Be Authentic: Genesis 25-50*, p. 73. Colorado Springs, CO: David C. Cook.

13. Keller, P. (2007) *A Shepherd Looks at Psalm 23*, p. 172. Zondervan.

14. Wiersbe, W. (1983) *Be Authentic: Genesis 25-50*, p. 82. Colorado Springs, CO: David C. Cook.

15. Guzik, D. (2008) *Genesis Commentary*. Goleta, CA: Enduring Word Media. Retrieved from enduringword.com.

16. *GotQuestions.com*. (n.d.). "Who Were the Edomites?" Retrieved from gotquestions.org/ Edomites.html.

17. Guzik, D. (2020) *Online Q&A with David Guzik*. Retrieved from enduringword.com/what-happened-to-the-edomites-live-qa-for-december-10-2020.

18. Thomas, I. (1961) *The Saving Life of Christ*, p. 90-91. Grand Rapids, MI: Zondervan.

19. Briscoe, J. (1987) *The Communicator's Commentary: Genesis*, p. 300-301. Waco, TX: World Books.

20. Thomas, I. (1961) *The Saving Life of Christ*, p. 83-84. Grand Rapids, MI: Zondervan.

21. Wiersbe, W. (1983) *Be Authentic: Genesis 25-50*, p. 83. Colorado Springs, CO: David C. Cook.

22. Thomas, I. (1961) *The Saving Life of Christ*, p. 92-93. Grand Rapids, MI: Zondervan.